Worldwide human trafficking is
justice and neighbor-love in the ...... p------ ,
prophetic call to the church to move realistically to counter it. God,
give us ears to hear Eddie Byun's word for our times.

J.I. Packer
Author of *Knowing God* and Professor of Theology at Regent College

Biblically informed, practical, and ultimately shaped by the Gospel,
A Light in Darkness illumines a profound failure in the evangelical
church: once again forgetting that justice is at the heart of bearing
God's name and image in the world. Read this prayerfully. Read this
carefully. Ultimately, ask the Lord to lead you into his ways in this
present evil age. A profoundly important message for the church today.

Kyle Strobel
**Co-author of *The Way of the Dragon or the Way of the Lamb:
Searching for Jesus' Path of Power in a Church that has Abandoned It.***

I have been blessed to know Dr. Eddie Byun for the past five years.
During this time, Dr. Byun has helped bring crucial awareness on
this issue to our campus. He was instrumental in helping ignite a
flame for justice in our school and guiding our student ministries. He
lives and breathes by the power of the Holy Spirit to bring awareness
and action plans to battle this worldwide evil. His life is a testimony
of bringing light in the darkness.

Dr. Terry Franson
Senior Vice President Emeritus, Azusa Pacific University

Eddie's book is instructive, insightful, and impactful. Indeed, Eddie
powerfully and accurately captures God's heart and instructions on
biblical justice, especially involving vulnerable women and children.
What is also special about Eddie is that he "walks the talk" on biblical justice. Eddie's book, as well as his life, will enlighten, encourage,
and empower you. His book is a must-read.

Mark del Mundo
Lawyer and Co-Founder of Restore Children and Family Services

Eddie Byun opens our eyes to the realities of human trafficking
around the world. *A Light in Darkness* is the fruit of years of experience and a pastor's personal journey of engaging in the fight against
modern slavery. Byun offers biblical and practical counsel to help
us and our churches embody God's passion for the most vulnerable.

Uche Anizor
**Associate Professor of Theology, Talbot School of Theology,
Biola University**

Whether your church wants to be educated about human trafficking, gain a biblical perspective concerning it, or is seeking practical means to combat the evil, *A Light in Darkness* is a must-read. I have known Eddie for many years and his ministries have always been on the cutting edge of fighting human trafficking. In this book, he gives the Church proven methods to answer God's command to stand with the oppressed and fight injustice.

Don Brewster
Founder of Agape International Missions

Everyone loves the idea of justice...until there's a cost to justice. But the truth is there's always a cost to justice. Eddie calls the Church to pursue justice - not because it's trendy - but because God loves justice and hates injustice. This book walks us through the path of seeking justice.

Eugene Cho
Pastor of Quest Church and Founder of One Day's Wages

A LIGHT IN DARKNESS

A LIGHT IN DARKNESS

The Church's Role in Ending Human Trafficking

EDDIE BYUN

We enjoy hearing from our readers. Please contact
us at www.anekopress.com/questions-comments
with any questions, comments, or suggestions.

www.eddiebyun.com

A Light in Darkness

© 2023 by Eddie Byun

All rights reserved. First edition 2014.

Second edition 2023.

Cover Designer: Jonathan Lewis

Editors: Sheila Wilkinson and Ruth Clark

Aneko Press

www.anekopress.com

Aneko Press, Life Sentence Publishing, and our logos are trademarks of

Life Sentence Publishing, Inc.

203 E. Birch Street

P.O. Box 652

Abbotsford, WI 54405

RELIGION / Christian Living / Social Issues

Paperback ISBN: 978-1-62245-919-3

eBook ISBN: 978-1-62245-920-9

10 9 8 7 6 5 4 3 2 1

Available where books are sold

CONTENTS

Dedication...ix

Acknowledgments...xi

Introduction: My Journey... xiii

Ch. 1: Exposing the Darkness of Modern-Day Slavery 1

Ch. 2: Grounded in the Gospel 19

Ch. 3: A Biblical Foundation of Justice 29

Ch. 4: The Kingdom Value of Vulnerability 43

Ch. 5: Where Is the Justice of God? 55

Ch. 6: Why the Church Must Lead 71

Ch. 7: Freedom Sunday – Practicing Sabbath Justice..................87

Ch. 8: What the Church Can Do...97

Conclusion: The Time Is Now...133

Appendix 1: Resources for Freedom and Justice 139

Appendix 2: Case Study on Korea 143

About the Author..157

DEDICATION

To my Lord and Savior Jesus Christ who set this captive free from the greatest bondage of all.

To my wonderful wife, Hyun. I love you and thank God for you.

To my daughter, Emma, who is in the presence of Jesus. I can't wait to see you again.

To my son, Enoch. I am so happy you are my son.

ACKNOWLEDGMENTS

Thank you, Jesus, for your grace in saving me and the honor to serve you as I serve your people. Thank you, Hyun, for being so gracious, loving, and faithful. You are an amazing wife and mother. Thank you to my parents for their love and support throughout my life. Thank you, Charse Yun, for lending your gifts of editing and detailing to help with this project.

Thank you to Jeremiah Zeiset and the amazing team at ANEKO Press for your partnership in the gospel and believing in this project. Thank you to the phenomenal editing team at ANEKO (Sheila, Ruth, and Jeremiah). Your care for detail in grammar and especially theology was a blessing to see.

Thank you to the pastoral and administrative staff at Onnuri English Ministry who joined me on this journey of faith and obedience in Korea many years ago: Joel Yoon, Michael Lee, Isaac Surh, Daniel Park, Buri Suk, Mira Ahn, Estella Kang, JC Park, Mike Kim, Jane Kim, Eunji Kim, Andy Hodges, David Chung, Eunice Yun, Don Sutton, Stephanie Kim, Liz Linssen, Lisa Pak, and Sonia Yim.

Thank you to the amazing intercessors of OEM, especially Hannah Biggs, Kate Derbisire, Iman Lu, Christine Kim, Judy Kim, Izabel Orendain, Jonathan Miller, Mira Miller, Elisa Lee,

Gladys Figueroa, Mimi Song, Richard Biggs, Julie Brown, and Elizabeth Lee. Thank you to all of the OEM family for taking these steps of faith with me. Thank you to the HOPE Be Restored team for pioneering this justice ministry. Thank you, Jonathan English, Gracie Kim, and Jacob Bennett. Thank you, Onnuri Community Church, Pastor Ha Yong Jo, the Onnuri Women's Ministry, CGNTV, the Christian CEO Forum, Elder Philip Choi, and Duranno Publishing.

Thank you to the faculty, staff, and students at Torch Trinity Graduate University, especially to my students who pioneered our Freedom and Justice Course together. Thank you to all the Agape International Missions pastors for their love and support, especially David and Judy Hwang, Christian and Erin Lee, and Doug Park. Thank you, Handong Global University, Handong International Law School, Christ Bible Institute of Japan, and New Life Community Church.

Thank you, David Batstone and the Not for Sale family who opened my eyes to the injustice of human trafficking. Thank you to my fellow abolitionists Benji Nolot, Tara Teng, Don Brewster, Annie Dieselberg, NightLight International, Rahab Ministries, Thailand, Exodus Cry, International Justice Mission, Ratanak International, Unearthed, Voice of the Voiceless, Ecogender, Durebang, Dashihamke, Saenal, Women's Hope Center, Restore Children and Family Services in Cebu, and House of Hope for partnering together in our fight for freedom and justice in Korea and across the nations.

Thank you, Eddie Kim, Pat Yoon, KJ Lee, Bobby Lee, Midwest Youth Group, and Philadelphia Church of Vancouver. Thank you also to Jayesslee, Brian Joo, Danny Jung, Tim Hwang, and Jennifer Chung for supporting our justice conferences with your talents. Thank you to my colleagues and friends at Talbot School of Theology and Biola University.

INTRODUCTION: MY JOURNEY

Learn to do good; seek justice, correct oppression; bring justice to the fatherless, plead the widow's cause. (Isaiah 1:17)

There are more than fifty million slaves in the world today.[1]

"Nothing in the world is more dangerous than sincere ignorance and conscientious stupidity."[2]

A HOLY DISCONTENT

My heart was unusually restless. It was late afternoon in Seoul, and outside the sun was already low in the sky. Traffic would soon start the evening crawl. I had been a pastor for over fourteen years (in the United States, Canada, Australia, and South Korea) and loved what God had called me to do. I loved the preaching. I loved the discipleship. I loved shepherding the flock that was under my care. I loved sharing the gospel

---

1   Madeline Fitzgerald, "How Modern Slavery Survives Across the World," *U.S. News* (Dec. 15, 2022): *https://tinyurl.com/yc5nbfpj* (March 21, 2023).

2   Martin Luther King, Jr., Draft of Chapter IV, "Love in Action," *The Martin Luther King, Jr. Research and Education Institute* (July 1, 1962 to March 1, 1963): *https://tinyurl.com/yckse22v* (March 21, 2023).

with those who did not know Jesus. But for some reason, in the summer of 2010, I just couldn't shake a holy discontent that lingered in my heart. I sensed that God wanted me to do something else, but I just couldn't put my finger on it. I prayed. I asked God why I felt this way. Did He want me to move to a different city? Did He want me to change occupations? Did He want us to change the way we ministered? I wasn't sure, but I definitely knew things weren't supposed to stay the same.

Summer turned to fall. I continued to seek the Lord in prayer, but the restlessness of that evening continued to bother me. I didn't know why. Then one day, God gave me a word – two words, actually – *community transformation*. I had no idea what that meant. Did God want me to evangelize more? Were we supposed to serve our neighborhood more? What exactly did *community transformation* mean? I sought the Lord for more clarity, but didn't receive any other instruction – at least not at that time. For the next few months, I had the words *community transformation* in my prayer journal, but didn't know how to continue from there. If God wasn't going to give me any more information, I just had to trust that He would show me at the right time.

AWAKENING

Each year, our ministry chose a theme for the year. As 2010 came to a close, the theme God gave us for 2011 was "freedom." Just as I wasn't quite sure what *community transformation* meant for us, I wasn't sure what *freedom* would mean for our ministry either. Maybe God wanted us to experience personal break-throughs or deliverance from addictions in our lives. Perhaps it would mean that many people would come to know Christ and be set free from their sins. Regardless, I was excited to see how the new year would unfold.

In November of 2010, as our church prepared to celebrate Thanksgiving, I was given a copy of the book *Not for Sale* by David Batstone, which was my first introduction to human trafficking and modern-day slavery. Until that point, I had no idea slavery still existed in the world. I had heard of drug trafficking and arms trafficking, but not human trafficking. More out of curiosity than anything else, I opened that book on a cold November evening, and for the next few hours, my world was rocked.

My hands tightened as I gripped the book's pages. My emotions were growing more intense with each page. I recall the shock and anger that arose as I read about the plight of millions of people around the world who were bought and sold as commodities, and denied their human rights, dignity, and honor. Young Thai girls whose innocence was stolen as men violated them ten to twenty times per night. Boys in Uganda who were forced to kill their own parents and fight in wars rather than play with their friends and attend school.

The reality hit me like a bolt of lightning. God's message became clear for the first time since that restless visitation. I had prayed for guidance, for an answer. I had it now. In light of what I had read about the evils of modern-day slavery, the words *community, transformation,* and *freedom* all came together. Finally, I had a focus for all of the restlessness, the holy discontent that God had placed within me.

Almost every country in the world bears the stain of modern-day slavery, with millions of victims worldwide. Millions! In disbelief, I shook my head. How could there be so much evil and injustice in the world and I had never heard of any of it?

Every eight seconds someone is sold into slavery. Up to thirty million people are in slavery around the world. The U.S. Department of State estimates that there are 600,000 to 800,000 children, women, and men trafficked across international borders annually.[3] One study estimates that in South Korea alone, there are over one million South Korean women who are forced into sexual servitude. This multi-billion-dollar industry affects every nation in the world. The world of human trafficking is well networked from law enforcement to immigration to travel agents to taxi drivers.

What drives the sex-trafficking industry's demand? In a nutshell, lust and greed. The lust of the flesh is so self-centered and uncontrollable that customers and "johns" have become slaves to their own desires, and the traffickers' greed fuels this industry. Their greed has blinded them to the value and dignity of human life. Greed eventually leads the trafficker to commit the heinous crime of selling people as property. The uncontrollable desire for more wealth has destroyed the trafficker's conscience, causing him to regard human life as property to buy and sell.

Scripture warns us of the corrupting dangers of greed:

- *For the love of money is a root of all kinds of evils.* (1 Timothy 6:10)

- *You shall not pervert justice. You shall not show partiality, and you shall not accept a bribe, for a bribe blinds the eyes of the wise and subverts the cause of the righteous.* (Deuteronomy 16:19)

Human trafficking is one of the darkest manifestations of sin. When you hear the stories of these women and children who have been subjected to starvation, rape, physical beatings, mental manipulation, and inadequate living conditions, having their lives, dreams, and dignity stolen from them, you realize that what has happened to these precious souls is nothing short of evil. For many, life as a slave is the closest thing to hell on earth that anyone can experience.

That's the thing about this particular evil: we can't see it for what it is. Evil would like to keep us in the dark, blind to injustice. When we take a step back and look at the extent to

---

3   Louise Shelley, *Human Trafficking: A Global Perspective* (New York: Cambridge University Press, 2010), 5.

which modern-day slavery has spread to almost every country on the planet, we are forced to see it for what it truly is: massive, systemically global and pervasive, and truly evil.

And that is how God defines *injustice* in His Word. He calls it evil.

> *"You shall not spread a false report. You shall not join hands with a wicked man to be a malicious witness. You shall not fall in with the many to do evil, nor shall you bear witness in a lawsuit, siding with the many, so as to pervert justice, nor shall you be partial to a poor man in his lawsuit."* (Exodus 23:1-3)

Injustice is evil in the sight of God, and I was seeing it in one of its worst forms.

I set the book down on my desk. The stories had shaken me to my core, and my blood was boiling. I was outraged, and I knew I had to do something. But what? As a pastor, I wondered what my congregation could do. I did an online search to find churches that had ministries to combat trafficking, so that I could get my church on board with this fight for justice. Unfortunately, my search came up empty. Many churches had ministries to serve the poor and to help the orphans of the world, but I couldn't find a ministry that was trying to bring an end to this great evil of human trafficking in our day. Regardless, I knew without a shadow of a doubt that we, as a church, had to do something.

With no precedent before me and with no books on how the church can fight human trafficking to guide me, I got on my knees and prayed once again. "God, I am so angry at all the injustices that I just read about. I cannot believe this is happening, and I know Your heart breaks too. God, what can I do? What can our church do? Guide us, lead us, and use us for Your glory to bring forth justice in our day."

As I prayed, I kept a pen and a pad of paper next to me. I like to "brainstorm" with God. I pray and wait for God to speak. I leave room for God to give me inspiration, ideas, and insights on Scripture and on anything else He would have me do. That night, the ideas started to flow.

A CHURCH AWAKENING

With each new idea that God was giving me, my heart pounded faster and faster in excitement with the realization that we finally had a game plan to attack this evil of human trafficking. By the end of the year, a passion for justice burned in my heart, but this was not yet on the radar for my church. I had an action plan, but had no one to join me in this battle – yet. So at the start of the new year of "freedom," I preached on God's heart for justice and the plight of millions who are in slavery both physically and spiritually around the world. We started a new ministry called HOPE Be Restored and began monthly meetings where we would pray, learn, strategize, and plan our next steps towards justice. We hosted two conferences that first year to educate and equip our people as to what was happening and what we could do to stop it.

We sent short-term missions teams to Thailand and Cambodia to work with local organizations on the front lines of rescuing children and restoring dignity to their lives. For weeks at a time, we prayed, fasted, and gave money to various anti-human-trafficking organizations. We went on regular prayer walks around red-light districts (RLDs) and other known trafficking hotspots. By God's grace, after several months of intercession, some of these establishments began to close. Some may dismiss it as a coincidence, but I've discovered that the more you pray, and the more specifically you pray, the more "coincidences" occur in life. Suddenly, a fire for justice spread throughout our church, and an army was rising up.

I encouraged our congregation – many of them expats and foreign teachers – not to simply return home when their contracts were over, but to also consider using their gifts in countries where the gospel was needed and where vulnerable groups cried out for justice. As we took steps of faith and obedience as a church, many started to live lives of radical obedience in their pursuit of God. Some of the fruit of this period allowed us to see thirteen people become missionaries to spread the gospel and establish justice; nine people went to seminary, and four people went to law school. A number of our church members chose to get jobs as teachers in Thailand, Cambodia, Saudi Arabia, and Kuwait, specifically to be in a place where they could be an agent of change in the fight against human trafficking. As their pastor, I was so proud of them.

Here are a few testimonies from that special season of ministry:

JASON G.

I first heard about human trafficking and modern-day slavery when I was in college. Unfortunately, I didn't fully understand the issue, and I thought modern-day slavery referred to poor, starving kids in Africa. To be honest, at that time I didn't care, and I went on with my life. A few years later, I moved to Korea and became involved in a church, Onnuri English Ministry (OEM). It was the first time in my life that I had ever heard a sermon about justice. More importantly, justice wasn't simply a sermon series that we listened to for a few weeks at a Sunday service. Justice became a vital part of who we were as a church. From conferences to missions trips to prayer walks, the church became increasingly exposed to the realities of God's heart for justice.

I went on a missions trip with OEM to visit Agape International Missions (AIM) in Cambodia. It was during this short-term missions trip that God confronted me with the question, Will you go where you don't want to go? Will you stay where you don't want to stay? God had finally convinced me: Justice isn't optional. It must be a part of the DNA of His church.

This awakening to justice that began in Korea led me to pursue my master of arts degree in justice and mission, begin a human-trafficking prayer group at my church, and create the Colorado Justice Coalition. Going forward, I am in the process of establishing a full-time human-trafficking ministry in Colorado.

STEVEN M.

The trajectory of my life was completely changed by the work that God was doing in Korea through Onnuri English Ministry, and I remember clearly the moment that it all began. It was in early 2011 during the first major event that OEM hosted on the subject of justice and human trafficking. For quite some time before that, God had been placing on my heart a desire to help those less fortunate than myself, although I really had no idea in what capacity that could be. Over the course of that weekend, God touched a deep nerve in my soul. When Pastor Eddie asked members of the church to commit to God's work, I quickly stood because I knew God was calling me to do that. And when I heard about the need for skilled people to help as a first choice in life, I felt again that He was talking directly to me.

After that weekend, I got involved in helping to build OEM's human-trafficking ministry in whatever ways I could, from fasting to praying to short-term missions trips with my wife. I didn't know where it would all lead me, but over time, I felt God's push to leave Korea and move to Los Angeles to pursue a degree in law. It's funny because, had you asked me only a few months earlier, I would have told you that the last place I ever thought I'd live would be Los Angeles, and the last thing I would ever want to be was a lawyer. Yet here I am. I finished law school and am awaiting the results of the California bar exam. As before, I still don't know quite where God will ultimately lead me, but thanks to the work that He began during my time at OEM, I do know that the fight for justice will always be a central part of His purpose for my life.

APRIL R.

Human trafficking did not become evident to me until I had moved to Seoul, South Korea. I used to walk through a neighborhood that felt dark, heavy, and oppressed. Later I learned it was a red-light district. I remember constantly wondering how I could help when I didn't even speak the language. I prayed for guidance on how to minister to those in need.

There was a stirring in my soul, and Pastor Eddie preached about the very things that had been on my heart for over a year. Over the next eighteen months, I was challenged to participate in prayer walks, to pray and fast at home, to fast to give to those in need, and to tell others in person or via social media. I learned that even though I did not speak the language, there were things that I could do. I learned that prevention is an important part in combating trafficking. As a teacher, I wanted to use my skills to fight for justice by helping those who had little to no education. As a result of these convictions from God, I moved to New Delhi, India, with the goal of ministering to victims of human trafficking. After a season there, God led me to Mexico to serve the children there. The community where I lived is a high-risk area (low education, low income, single parents, high levels of sexual abuse and incest). I am compelled to do my part to help these young women strive for a life different from the one that surrounds them.

So how did the justice freedom movement change my life? I moved to India! Before learning about human trafficking, India was never on my radar. However, as I looked at the stats on human trafficking (both labor and sex) in India, I knew I could not stay in the comfort of my own country. Here was a country with millions of young boys and girls forced into slavery, and God called me to go. And I keep going wherever He sends me. After this year, I am prayerfully seeking a way to go to Thailand and continue in this path of seeking God's justice for the world.

A YEAR OF FREEDOM

With each step we took, everything became clearer. I finally understood what God meant when He gave our church the phrase, "community transformation." He was announcing that the upcoming ministry year would be one of freedom. It was clear. As a church, God wanted us to join the fight for freedom and combat the great evil of human trafficking in our community and around the world.

As the year progressed, it truly transformed into a year of freedom on so many levels. Our timing seemed to coincide with a global wave. Other organizations and churches appeared to be confirming a surge of concern about this issue. As the government made gestures toward cracking down on sex trafficking, laws were passed. Just as we got the biblical justice ball rolling in 2011, CNN announced The Freedom Project, promising to spotlight more stories on fighting human slavery. Although they were a secular news organization, they made me reflect on the role of the church in partnering with the cause (I talk more about this later). CNN even covered our Freedom Sunday service that year.

Not only did we assist in the freedom of people who had previously been enslaved in Korea and around the world, but also our church was set free to truly be the living body of Christ that it was meant to be. Our church came to life in ways I'd never seen before. We looked after the outcasts, and gave up our own food and money so that the poor could be fed. We were no longer concerned with ourselves but with loving our neighbors in the way that God intended His people to. The transformation was massive, but it also brought new challenges, including some resistance. But the overall momentum was too strong to ignore; this is where God was leading us.

WHAT CAN WE DO TO HELP?

Our congregation had undergone a genuine transformation. Though we had our share of critics, thankfully most of the churches and pastors I met were encouraging. In fact, as more people learned about what we were doing, the most common question I would get is, What can my church do to help?

The biggest frustration I saw in others was not knowing what they could do as Christians to join the fight for freedom and justice around the world. Beyond simply donating money to other organizations, which is admirable, the question that kept coming up was, What could an individual or a church do to end human trafficking in our day and age?

Fortunately, my brainstorming sessions with God gave me a number of practical steps to recommend to others. This was one of the primary motivations for writing this book. I wanted to provide the church with practical steps for every person to become a part of the solution to this problem. Whatever your gifting is, use it to impact your sphere of influence. Whatever your passion is, use it to spread this message of justice for all. So write, paint, draw, speak, publish, compose, act, campaign, or anything else to the glory of God and for the good of others.

I want to give the church a practical guide on what individual believers and church communities can do to rise up and become change agents for the good of our cities and communities all over the world. It is my prayer that the fruit of this book will result in the freedom of the nations, and who knows, maybe even the freedom of some churches along the way as well.

GROUP DISCUSSION QUESTIONS:

- When did you first become aware of human trafficking and how did it make you feel?

- What do you know about human trafficking in your own community?

- Do you feel the church should be involved for freedom and justice around the world? Why or why not?

PRAYER GUIDE:

- Ask God to give you His heart of love, compassion, and justice as you read this book.

- Pray for your church to be a source of light and love to the community that you are in.

- Pray that the fruit of this study will lead to freedom in your nation.

CHAPTER 1

EXPOSING THE DARKNESS OF MODERN-DAY SLAVERY

"'Cursed be anyone who perverts the justice due to the sojourner, the fatherless, and the widow.' And all the people shall say, 'Amen.'" (Deuteronomy 27:19)

Human trafficking affects every country around the world, generating more than $32 billion worldwide.[4]

"Injustice anywhere is a threat to justice everywhere."[5]

M indy was the youngest daughter in a large family in a remote Thai village. She grew up knowing she had to support her parents, as is common with many young Thai girls born and raised in the countryside. In her case, she accepted the role of primary breadwinner for her family, so she looked for work in her hometown, but it was difficult because of the poverty.

---

4 "Combating human trafficking and modern-day slavery; Ten years of impact, 2002-2012," *Polaris Project: For a World Without Slavery: https://tinyurl.com/3atnbfvu* (March 21, 2023).

5 Martin Luther King, Jr., "Letter from Birmingham Jail," April 16, 1963, *Bill of Rights Institute: https://billofrightsinstitute.org/primary-sources/letter-from-birmingham-jail* (March 21, 2023).

Then one day, her uncle mentioned that he had a friend who could help her find work in the United States. Mindy had never ventured outside her village, but she decided to go and make the sacrifice for the sake of her family. With her uncle's help, she got her first passport and was overjoyed with it. She thought she would be able to make money for the family after all, and the future appeared to be bright. After her first time in an airplane, one of her uncle's friends helped her at Los Angeles International Airport. There, she met her boss.

At first, she worked as a waitress. Mindy was nervous. She didn't speak English, and the work was hard. Then her boss asked for her passport. "Just to keep things safe," he said. Mindy had no other choice but to trust him, so she handed over her passport.

The very next day, the boss came to Mindy. He told her, "You no longer work at the restaurant." He threw a new set of clothes at her and demanded she wear them. Mindy couldn't believe her eyes. The clothes were skimpy and promiscuous. As a shy girl from the country, she would never wear such clothes. When she refused, her boss hit her. Out of fear, she put on the clothes. After that, he violated her and continued to beat her. Mindy was humiliated, bruised, and in shock.

She started a new job the next day, hosting men who violated her every night. Despite living in the United States for two years, she had for the most part only seen the inside of hotel rooms. Every three days, she was transferred to a new city and hotel room. She was completely under her boss's control in this new land with nowhere to run to and no ability to communicate.

I wish this story was rare, but it isn't. This isn't just happening in Los Angeles and San Francisco but also in Shanghai and Seoul. This is the current state of human trafficking. Fortunately for Mindy, an undercover officer was able to apprehend her kidnapper. But unfortunately, there are many more Mindys enslaved in your own city today.

These women have names. They have stories. They have families. But as we read or hear about these women in the press, the temptation is to view them as faceless and nameless. A key first step in this battle against darkness is education – to make ourselves aware and informed. It is to know our enemy. This chapter seeks to expose evil by shining light into what seems like murky, chaotic darkness. I have to warn you; the sheer magnitude of the statistics and facts may overwhelm you. They will seem legion. Satan would prefer we remain blind to this overview of modern-day slavery and leave this information hidden and unknown. Girls like Mindy – and countless other women and children – will then remain forgotten, their names and lives cloaked in darkness, hidden from the world in sordid hotel rooms, brothels, and karaoke bars, never seeing the light of day.

Providing an overview of the contours of the problem means we boldly shed light into the darkness, revealing evil for what it really is and casting it out in Jesus' name – the name above all names.

In order to defeat evil, one of the first things we need to do is define the enemy. We need to assess their tactics, note their strength and troop movements, discover their battle plans, and identify their base camps (see Luke 14:28).

Let's assess an overview of the battlefield together.

THE BASICS

Here are some of the basics of human trafficking to begin with. These are the three main types of trafficking happening in the world today: arms trafficking, drug trafficking, and human trafficking.

Each of these industries is worth billions of dollars. Though arms trafficking is currently the most prevalent, human trafficking is the fastest-growing form of illegal enterprise worldwide. Selling bodies is a form of modern-day slavery and one of the most heinous crimes that has resurfaced in our generation.

There are estimates of more than 50 million slaves in our world today,[6] with well over one hundred thousand people enslaved in the United States alone.[7] Of these victims, 80 percent are female, 50 percent are minors, and 70 percent are trafficked for sexual exploitation.[8]

Human trafficking is happening on every continent of the world. The Trafficking In Persons (TIP) Report states that 12.3 million people worldwide are forced into bonded labor, child labor, and sexual servitude. The U.S. government reported that approximately 600,000 to 800,000 people were victims of trafficking worldwide. In Europe, there is an estimated 400,000 people entering Europe illegally each year.[9] Even a small and isolated country such as Iceland, with a population of only 250,000, has had trafficking cases reported.[10]

Human trafficking is crudely economical. Because of how lucrative it is and the relative ease of transport for their "goods," it has become the preferred choice of activity among organized crime groups these days. Transporting a person across international borders is much easier than transporting drugs or weapons, and the sale of a human life appears to be almost limitless in terms of profit. For instance, if you sell one gram of drugs, you can only sell it once. However, if you sell a person, you can sell that person again and again.

DEFINITION
Human trafficking is defined as the recruitment, harboring, transporting, providing, or obtaining of any person for forced labor, slavery, or servitude in any industry, including agriculture, construction, prostitution, and manufacturing.

---

6   Fitzgerald, "How Modern Slavery Survives Across the World" (February 24, 2023).
7   David Batstone, *Not for Sale: The Return of the Global Slave Trade—and How We Can Fight It* (New York: HarperCollins Publishers, 2010), 3.
8   Shelley, *Human Trafficking*, 5.
9   Ibid., 4.
10   Ibid., 2.

It can also involve smuggling – taking people across borders illegally, kidnapping – taking people against their will, coercion – forcing people through manipulation, rape, drugging, imprisonment, theft, forgery, or threat.

SOURCE, TRANSIT, AND DESTINATION COUNTRIES
Almost every country in the world has a recorded case of human trafficking, but each country's involvement differs. A country is known as either a source, a transit, or a destination in its connection with trafficking. A source country is where the victims come from, a destination country is where the victims end up, and a transit country is where they travel to get from source to destination. For example, South Korea is a major source country for sex-trafficking victims and a destination country for both sex trafficking and labor trafficking. It is also a transit country, bringing in people from all over Asia and Europe who end up in Japan, Australia, and the United States.

REASONS PEOPLE ARE TRAFFICKED

Several main arenas explain why human trafficking occurs.

LABOR EXPLOITATION
Sometimes people are trafficked to do manual labor within a given industry. Three main types of labor exploitation involve sweatshops, housework, and child labor.

The *sweatshop factory* setting requires people to work long hours with little or no pay. They are usually in an unsafe or unhealthy work environment, and it is not uncommon for these people to sleep, work, and live in the same cramped and overcrowded room with many others. Though the term *sweatshop factory* implies an indoor workplace, the type of labor required can also be outdoor work such as farming, brick-making, and other forms of slave labor. Another common factor is that they cannot leave their workplace on their own volition.

A frequent, though less recognized, form of labor exploitation is *housework*. This one is difficult to see or find because these individuals are within a home setting where they cannot leave. The households may appear to have regular maids, but they are not free to come and go as they please.

Child labor is another growing problem in the world of human trafficking, forcing children to work long, hard hours and usually without pay. These children are taken away from their families and not allowed to attend school or play with their friends. They are placed in unhealthy or dangerous work conditions. In some parts of Africa, children as young as eight are kidnapped and taken to cocoa farms to pick cocoa beans for fourteen to sixteen hours a day.[11] Sadly, much of the chocolate and coffee that we consume on a daily basis is the fruit of their suffering. In Nepal, children are trafficked to weave carpets because of their small fingers, which are more effective in weaving together the very small and detailed designs used on the carpets. Instead of enjoying life as a child, they labor and suffer under slave conditions.

MARRIAGES AND MAIL-ORDER BRIDES

Many women around the world are sold into marriages only to become slaves to their new "husbands" and families. For example, because of China's one-child policy and preference for males, many baby girls have been aborted throughout the years. This has led to a massive imbalance between men and women, with men outnumbering the women. This vacuum of Chinese women available for marriage to Chinese men has created a market to find women from abroad to become their

11 "Child Labor and Slavery in the Chocolate Industry" (January 2022), *Food Empowerment Project: https://foodispower.org/human-labor-slavery/slavery-chocolate/* (February 25, 2023).

wives. As a result, when North Korean refugees are caught crossing the border into China, the women are often tricked, trafficked, or forced into these types of marriages.

Hmong refugees are often imported to the United States as second wives for the Chinese men there.[12] In South Korea, the rural areas and farming communities are seeing a decrease in women available for these farmers to marry because most go to the big city in search of jobs. So mail-order brides are often bought from Southeast Asia (the Philippines, Vietnam, Cambodia, and Thailand), but once they arrive, they are treated as property – slaves – and often beaten and abused by their new husbands.

BEGGING
Tragically, children are trafficked and forced to beg wealthy tourists for money on the streets of various cities around the world. What these tourists don't realize is that these kids are beaten and not given food if they do not return with enough money for their owners. Others are mutilated in order to appear more helpless and gain sympathetic dollars from the visitors. In India, the "beggar mafia" will maim children on purpose to make them better-looking beggars, often with the help of doctors who will do the maiming for the right price.[13] Kids are intentionally blinded, limbs are removed, and handicapped children are left without food and water to get a dehydrated, desperate appearance.

CHILD SOLDIERS
Another very disturbing evil that is affecting children in different parts of the world is child warriors. UNICEF (United Nations International Children's Emergency Fund) estimates that over three hundred thousand children younger than eighteen are trafficked to serve in armed conflicts worldwide.[14] In

---

12   Shelley, *Human Trafficking*, 64.
13   Ibid.
14   Ibid., 5.

Africa and Latin America, these child soldiers are ordered to fight in horrific wars. They are not only forced to bear arms, but they are also forced to kill their own family members in order to cut off any emotional ties to the world around them. After being traumatized by the violence, the young boys are trained to kill, rape, and mutilate their victims, while girls are taken to be sex slaves for older men in the army.

ORGAN TRAFFICKING

The very rich, very sick people (in every sense of the word) who are in desperate need of organ transplants but cannot wait in line are the driving force of this market. The victims are often very poor men and women who do not intend to give up their organs. A host of problems arise with organ trafficking. The victims are usually forced to give up their organs even without any payment, and because of the illegal nature of this, the procedure is usually done in unsanitary conditions, leaving serious health issues for the victims to deal with afterwards, such as infections or even death. The World Health Organization (WHO) estimates that 10 percent of all seventy thousand kidneys used for transplants each year are obtained on the black market.[15]

ADOPTION AND ORPHANS

Children are also trafficked for adoption from the developing world, primarily Latin America, Russia, and Asia, to parents in North America and Western Europe who pay high fees to get these babies. In Southeast Asia, France, Greece, and Bulgaria, pregnant women have been trafficked to secure their babies even from birth. "Orphan tourism" exists in Cambodia and other poor countries that promote "tourist specials" for visiting an orphanage. They take photos of these children and horrifically and sexually exploit them for a few dollars.

---

15   Shelley, *Human Trafficking*, 75.

SEXUAL EXPLOITATION

Sex trafficking is by far the more prevalent reason human trafficking happens today. The victims are not just women either. Men, women, boys, and girls are all victims of this injustice. It may take the common form of prostitution on the streets, but it can also be disguised in the form of karaoke bars, massage parlors, nail salons, and a host of other practices where people pay to violate the bodies of these victims.

Indeed, several of our team members have reported being utterly shocked that the respectable neighborhoods they live in here in Seoul have massage parlors and brothels tucked around the corner. Elizabeth Lee was completely shocked to see that the hundreds of cards littering her neighborhood in Seoul where she came home from work and where children walked to school every day weren't advertisements for the local hair salon. These were openly advertising prostitution.

One day, after Elizabeth and our team prayed outside of an RLD, she saw a taxicab pull up. She said, "A middle-aged Korean man stepped out. He went down the alley to one of the brothels closest to the street. He walked in, and then a few minutes later, he returned to the cab with a big envelope of money. Inside the taxicab, his elementary-school-aged son was waiting. And that was when I realized the depth of depravity. I saw how the sex industry wasn't isolated to madams, pimps, women, or johns. Rather, I saw that it affected families. My heart sank as I thought about the younger generation and what they would be growing into."

WHO ARE THE VICTIMS?

WOMEN

Women and girls are the most trafficked group in all the world. They account for 80 percent of all human-trafficking victims. Trafficking most frequently occurs in societies where women lack property rights, cannot inherit land, and do not enjoy equal protection under the law.[16] But it happens in nations where women have rights too. According to the U.S. Attorney General's report on trafficking in 2006, South Koreans accounted for the highest population (24 percent) of sex-trafficking victims in the United States. The popularity of Korean pop culture around the world with their girl bands dressed specifically to showcase their long legs, as well as Korean dramas that are now more popular in Southeast Asia than Hollywood movies, has created a high demand for Korean women in brothels all around the world. There are even cases of this in developed nations such as the United States and the United Kingdom.

This reveals the complex nature of global sex trafficking. It's often assumed that the victims of sex trafficking come from the poorest countries, but as we can see, South Korea, which has roughly the same per capita gross domestic product (GDP) as Italy and is considered a wealthy and developed country, is a major source country for sex trafficking. Clearly, there are complex push-and-pull factors that crisscross international boundaries. In Japan, another affluent and developed nation, there is the tragic phenomenon of *enjo kōsai,* where young Japanese teenagers date older men, often exchanging sex for money to buy luxury items such as designer purses. For many South Korean women, debt bondage is a major factor in pushing women to seek money overseas. Incurring large amounts of debt, they travel overseas only to find that they are preyed upon by immoral brokers who only add to their already huge debt. With their passports and status taken from them, many become trapped in the cycle of human trafficking. Some have tried to argue that many of these Korean women would not classify as victims of trafficking because they voluntarily left their country, lured by the prospect of a job by shady brokers. Once abroad, however, they cannot leave.

---

16   Shelley, *Human Trafficking,* 54.

CHILDREN

Many children in third-world countries are particularly susceptible to traffickers who use them for labor and sexual exploitation.[17] Though child prostitution is illegal all over the world, estimates say there are over two million children who are forced into the global sex trade. Many men, for fear of HIV and diseases in older women, prefer having sex with children since they are less likely to carry any disease. Virginity is highly valued in some cultures, with men willing to pay high sums of money for a child who is still a virgin. In fact, in some cultures, people think that having sex with a virgin will cure them of certain diseases like AIDS, creating a higher demand for younger and younger children. Not only do the children become infected with diseases, but some also end up addicted to drugs that the trafficker supplies to them. Others get pregnant, and most are malnourished. If intervention does not happen soon, they will face an early death. It is child abuse in one of its worst forms.

MEN

Men are also trafficked, but primarily for forced manual labor or to work on fishing boats. Due to a debt that the man must pay off or threats to the safety of his family, the victim has little choice but to live life as a slave until someone can help set him free. In India, some men are paying off past generations of debt that began with the father or even the grandfather. The cycle often continues as children who are born during this time of slavery will inherit the debt incurred by the parents. From an early age, they are raised into thinking that slavery is their identity.

THE STATELESS

The TIP Report estimated that twelve million people are stateless around the world. Stateless people have no legal proof of citizenship,

---

17   Shelley, *Human Trafficking*, 52.

so they are unable to register a birth, educate their children, get health care, work, or even travel legally. They have no protection from police or government or legal systems, which leave them incredibly vulnerable to traffickers.[18] They are one of the most vulnerable groups in all the world. Many stateless people can be found among the hill tribes of Northern Thailand, the Roma people in Europe, and the Haitian migrants in the Caribbean. A growing number of stateless children emerged recently in South Korea.

Migrant workers from Southeast Asia have children with U.S. military men, but the men leave the country and leave undocumented children in their wake. Without the support of their father, neither the United States, nor South Korea, nor even the mother's home country will give the child citizenship. Thus, thousands of children are left stateless and vulnerable.

Some surveys have estimated that of all the women working the red-light districts in Thailand, over 80 percent are stateless females from a northeast region called Isaan. Because they are stateless, the only working visa the Thai government gives them is to work in the sex industry. If that is the case, is it really a choice? One small ray of light is that the Thai government will give citizenship to the stateless if they graduate with a university degree. This opens up a whole new world of opportunities for them. Upon learning about this, our church created scholarships to help stateless children in Thailand attend university and never allow finances to be a reason for not finishing.

In a similar way, refugees are left vulnerable to a government that will not provide safety and shelter for them. The dangerous plight of North Korean refugees who cross over from their nightmare in North Korea into China is that they will not always have a better life waiting for them. Many North Korean refugees in China end up being sold as unwilling brides or are trafficked for sex throughout the world.

18   Shelley, *Human Trafficking,* 51.

THE POOR

Those who are poor or are paying off large amounts of debt become vulnerable to the world of sex trafficking. Those who need large sums of money will fall prey to loan sharks who charge astronomical amounts of interest that the debtors are unable to pay.[19] Many women who end up in the sex industry in South Korea are victims of this type of debt bondage. Sometimes, through credit card debt or high medical bills due to sudden health crises within their family, they need large amounts of money in a short amount of time. They are unable to get a legitimate loan through the bank, so they turn to loan sharks who enslave them to work in the sex industry to pay off their debts.

THE ORPHAN

In Moldova and other parts of Europe are known cases where orphanage staff partner with traffickers and tell them when girls will "age out" of the orphanage. They connect them with "lover boys" who pose as interested boyfriends, only to sell them to traffickers once the girls buy into the lie of the boyfriends' love. Sadly, because no one has adopted them and cares for them, many will disappear once they leave the system. With no family, there is no one who knows when they go missing.

CAUSES

Depending on whom you talk to, there are various reasons human trafficking is spreading around the world. From a political and economic standpoint, some will say *globalization* is the cause, where the disparity between the rich and poor is ever widening. "The supply exists because globalization has caused increasing economic and demographic disparities between the developing world and the developed world, along with the feminization of poverty and the marginalization of many

---

19   Shelley, *Human Trafficking*, 57.

rural communities."[20] Along those lines, the lack of employment opportunities and increasing poverty are the reasons this exists. From a sociological perspective, a low view of women and children is seen as the cause. "Women and female children are particularly vulnerable to trafficking because of their low social status and the lack of investment in girls."[21]

Yet digging deeper, there is another common cause for all the trafficking that happens around the world: corruption. At each stage, deep levels of corruption are involved. Sometimes it is the local law enforcement being paid to look the other way; in other cases, it's the immigration officers. In these places, endemic corruption in the justice systems of the world is what seems to allow this injustice to run rampant.

But more than a product of political, economic, or even sociological factors, we must see human trafficking for what it truly is – a great moral evil that has corrupted the heart. It is a spiritual issue at its core, which is why the church must be involved. If we boil it down to its lowest common denominators, we will see that greed and lust are the driving forces of this evil around the world. The love of money is a root of all kinds of evil, and we see the seed of greed result in the weeds of wickedness all around us. Profits from sex exploitation each year are over $33.9 billion![22]

ONE SOLUTION

In light of such evil, what can be done? Our efforts seem so puny in the face of such staggering sums.

In February 2013, we invited Don Brewster and his wife, Bridget, the founders of Agape International Missions, to speak at our Justice Conference. The couple moved to Cambodia in

---

20   Shelley, *Human Trafficking*, 2.
21   Ibid., 16.
22   Shelley, *Human Trafficking*, 7.

2006 and later founded Rahab's House, which provides out-reach, education, and aid for sex-trafficking victims.

Like many of you, some of us questioned whether any of our small, individual efforts could make a difference in light of the enormity of evil. But as Don reminded us, Jesus is the one who leaves the ninety-nine to go after the one.

Don told us the story of what he calls "The One" – a tough Cambodian girl named Srey Leak. Srey Leak was born in 1996, but she's seen more horror than most adults ever will. She came to Rahab's House at a time when they simply didn't have the money or resources to take on one more person. To do so would have put the other girls under the Brewsters' care in jeopardy. It was an added burden and a financial risk. As for Srey Leak, she wasn't interested in any kind of shelter. She was broke, without any food or money. Sure, the job was tough, but money was the solution, right? And if so, how could Rahab's House possibly help her?

Like many others, Srey Leak came from a broken family background. Her father was an alcoholic who regularly beat her. Srey Leak ran away from home, alone on the streets of Phnom Penh, and like so many young girls, she ended up in the sex trade where she underwent horrific abuse and torture. She lost her innocence at the hands of cruel men who exploited her young teenaged body for sheer profit. She bounced from one karaoke bar to another before ending up in the notorious Svay Pak area.

Now, you might wonder why Srey Leak didn't go back home. But in Cambodia, there is a saying: *Boys are like gold and girls are like cloth.* Once soiled, the cloths are good for nothing. They become dirty rags. Srey Leak really believed this. She felt that she had no other choice in life but to work in karaoke bars. This is the world that lies and says that your value and worth depend on what little money and scraps you can get – even if it means selling your body and your soul.

But in following Jesus, Don decided to focus on the one – this special daughter of Christ – despite the lack of money. The Brewsters took her in. What a difference! The greedy brothel kicked her out because Srey Leak had gotten pregnant twice (she was forced to abort both babies) and was producing no money for them. The Brewsters took her in even though they had no money for the next month.

But when Srey Leak first came to Rahab's House, she had no intention of staying. She resisted every step of the way. But the staff doctor examined Srey Leak's incredibly damaged body and told her she needed proper medication and rest. She reluctantly agreed to spend the night.

That first night for Srey Leak was long. Lights-out at Rahab's House is 9:00 p.m. Srey Leak's night usually started then and didn't end till five o'clock in the morning. But the other girls were nice to her. Srey Leak was amazed by their kindness. At first, Srey Leak thought this was "cool." The next day, she was asked to help out with the kids' Bible camp. She hated kids, but to her own surprise, she discovered an emotion she hadn't felt in years – joy.

A few more weeks went by. The food was okay and the girls were nice, but Srey Leak had no interest in going to church or attending the morning Bible study that the girls kept inviting her to. She preferred to sleep in.

Eventually the love of Rahab's House won her over. Don and his staff continued to focus on this one girl, pouring out love to her in the littlest of ways. One day she announced, "I want to learn more about Jesus . . . and I want to know more about those heavenly things."

Srey Leak started going to morning Bible study. Two weeks later, she accepted Christ. Two days after Christmas, she was baptized. Now she works with the other rescued girls in making bracelets and jewelry, and she even joined the worship team. She says, "I can make a good living, and I have honor now." For the first time in her life, Srey Leak had value and respect.

As Don Brewster said, "I wish that we could look inside her heart to see the *true* transition, to really be able to see inside someone's heart who thinks they are a worthless piece of trash. To be transformed and believe that God wants them, that God loves them, that He cherishes them so that they are driven to worship Christ and lead others to do it is a miracle."

In light of such glory, words fail. Yes, our actions can make cataclysmic differences in the spiritual realms. I believe all the heavens rocked with joy as they celebrated Srey Leak's rescue, and darkness shuddered, cowered, and fled at the power and light emanating from Srey Leak's transformed life.

As Srey Leak's story shows, the driving force behind sex trafficking, which is the largest form of human trafficking today, is the lust of the flesh in the hearts of men and women around the world. Romans 1 reveals that hearts and minds grow darker the more we reject God and refuse to honor Him as God. The fundamental cause of the evil of human trafficking is a spiritual cause. And Srey Leak's salvation also shows that this spiritual problem is in need of a spiritual solution, which is why the church must take the lead in this battle. That is what we will discuss in the next chapter.

GROUP DISCUSSION QUESTIONS:

- Looking at the list of why people are trafficked, is there an area that gripped your heart more than others? Share.

- Are you interested in researching for yourself the presence of trafficked humans in your community? Looking at the list of who the victims of trafficking are, how many can be found within your own community?

- What do you believe to be the primary causes of the growth of trafficking in our day? What is the greatest need of these individuals as they are rescued?

PRAYER GUIDE:

- Pray through the list of people who are most vulnerable to trafficking and ask the Lord to protect them in your country and throughout the world.

- Pray for the children who are currently living in the nightmare of forced labor and sexual exploitation and ask the Lord to heal them and set them free even today.

- Pray for God's light to reveal injustices in your community and for those evils to be driven away.

CHAPTER 2

GROUNDED IN THE GOSPEL

Grace to you and peace from God our Father and
the Lord Jesus Christ, who gave himself for our sins
to deliver us from the present evil age, according
to the will of our God and Father, to whom be the
glory forever and ever. Amen. (Galatians 1:3-5)

During the pandemic, online recruitment (or
trafficking) increased significantly. Analysis
found an increase of 120 percent recruitment on
Facebook and 95 percent increase on Instagram.[23]

The test of a gospel-centered church is its doctrine on paper,
plus its culture in practice.[24] The gospel is at the heart of
justice and the abolition of slavery. We do this not simply because
it is a good thing to do, but also because it is a God-thing and a
godly thing to do. While some may refer to this type of ministry
as social justice, I want to emphasize that we do it because it is
biblical justice centered on the gospel of Jesus Christ.

---

23 "Sex Trafficking Statistics 2022 Worldwide (Research)," *Pressat* (February 8,
    2022): *https://tinyurl.com/45rkcw9b*.
24 Ray Ortlund, *The Gospel: How the Church Portrays the Beauty of Christ* (Wheaton:
    Crossway, 2014), 18.

One place to start looking at this through a gospel lens is in Paul's letter to the Galatians. In this pastoral letter, Paul wishes to ensure that this congregation does not stray from the one true gospel. He said,

> I am astonished that you are so quickly desert-
> ing him who called you in the grace of Christ and
> are turning to a different gospel—not that there is
> another one, but there are some who trouble you
> and want to distort the gospel of Christ. But even if
> we or an angel from heaven should preach to you a
> gospel contrary to the one we preached to you, let
> him be accursed. (Galatians 1:6-8)

This opening section of Galatians reminds us that the gospel is to be the center of our lives and the foundation of our ministries.

BECAUSE OF CHRIST CRUCIFIED, WE RECEIVE OUR ASSIGNMENT

One blessing we gain because of Christ crucified is that we receive our assignment. Paul begins his letter in Galatians by identifying who he is in relationship to Jesus Christ.

> Paul, an apostle—not from men nor through man,
> but through Jesus Christ and God the Father, who
> raised him from the dead—and all the broth-
> ers who are with me, To the churches of Galatia.
> (Galatians 1:1-2)

Paul identifies himself as an apostle, which means "one who is sent." To be an apostle, one needed to have seen Christ and to have been sent out by Him. This is a major theme of this let-ter. People had questioned his authority as an apostle and thus influenced the churches in Galatia to doubt his leadership and especially his gospel message. These false teachers were telling these new believers that they needed to be circumcised and be a good Jew first before becoming a Christian. As a result of this influence, much of his letter was a response to this false teaching.

So here, more than at any other time, Paul emphasizes the calling he received directly from Christ. Paul clarifies his calling in verse 1 as he states that his apostleship is *not from men nor through man, but through Jesus Christ and God the Father.* Jesus Christ directly called Paul into his apostolic service while on the road to Damascus. Then he states, *Through Jesus Christ and God the Father, who raised him from the dead.* The point of referring to the resurrection so early in this letter is to stress that the resurrection of Christ signified the new age of redemptive history. The old law of the Mosaic covenant is fulfilled in Christ. It is not about our work for God, but Christ's finished work for us when He died.

While we do not have to prove our position to others in the same way that Paul did, the call we have comes from Jesus Christ. We have our assignment today because of Christ crucified. Our authority as gospel preachers to our families, workplaces, and cities stems from the authority given to Christ by His resurrection. All that we are as a result of our faith in Christ is due to Christ crucified.

The cross of Jesus changes everything. Time is changed from BC to AD. Death is changed from a master to a servant. Eternity is changed for souls to rest with the Savior. Everything changed when Jesus died and rose from the grave. Who we are and what we are called to do both stem from what happened over two thousand years ago on Calvary.

Because of Christ crucified, we receive our assignment as messengers of the cross.

> *All this from God, who through Christ reconciled us*
> *to himself and gave us the ministry of reconciliation;*
> *that is, in Christ God was reconciling the world to*
> *himself, not counting their trespasses against them,*
> *and entrusting to us the message of reconciliation.*
> *Therefore, we are ambassadors for Christ, God mak-*
> *ing his appeal through us.* (2 Corinthians 5:18-20)

The cross is the centerpiece of our message. Paul declares later in this letter, *But far be it from me to boast except in the cross of our Lord Jesus Christ, by which the world has been crucified to me, and I to the world* (Galatians 6:14). And in 1 Corinthians 2:2, he states, *For I decided to know nothing among you except Jesus Christ and him crucified.* Paul's boast and his message was the cross of Jesus Christ. For without the cross, there is no crown. And without crucifixion, there is no resurrection. The cross is our message, and to declare it is our assignment.

BECAUSE OF CHRIST CRUCIFIED, WE RECEIVE OUR ATONEMENT

The cross has great significance and is cause for celebration. What does that mean in the life of a believer? We not only receive our assignment as messengers of grace, but we also receive our atonement as a result of His crucifixion. Paul continues his letter to the Galatians by saying, *Grace to you and peace from God our Father and the Lord Jesus Christ,* **who gave himself for our sins** (Galatians 1:3-4, emphasis added).

Only the cross of Jesus Christ could deal with our sin problem. At the cross, Jesus gave Himself for our sins. *For our sake he made him to be sin who knew no sin, so that in him we might become the righteousness of God* (2 Corinthians 5:21). This is the *atonement* of Christ, which simply means "made amends for." It is the Bible's central message.

Christ's work of atonement includes:

- His work of reconciliation (granting us peace with God).

- His work of propitiation (absorbing the wrath of God upon Himself).

- His work of penal substitution (taking our place of death and damnation).

- His work of complete forgiveness of all our sins.

Sin brings separation, but the death of Jesus tore the veil in two, giving us access to God again. Sin brings condemnation, but the death of Jesus restores our relationship with Him so that now there is no condemnation for those who are in Christ Jesus (Romans 8:1). Sin brings with it eternal damnation, but Christ came to give life with Him forevermore. These enormous blessings became available to us, all through the shedding of His blood on the cross.

Only the shed blood of Jesus can forgive our sins. *For the life of the flesh is in the blood, and I have given it for you on the altar to make atonement for your souls, for it is the blood that makes atonement by the life* (Leviticus 17:11). It is not enough for the sacrifice just to bleed; the sacrifice must also die through the shedding of its blood. *Indeed, under the law almost everything is purified with blood, and without the shedding of blood there is no forgiveness of sins* (Hebrews 9:22).

When Christ shed His blood, He poured out His very life to pay the eternally damning penalty for our sins, making us right with God. Because when God says that the wages of sin is death, He means it (Romans 6:23). Even though death killed Jesus on the cross, it is through the resurrection that Christ forever destroyed death's power!

"Death is swallowed up in victory." "O death, where is your victory? O death, where is your sting?" The sting of death is sin, and the power

*of sin is the law. But thanks be to God, who gives
us the victory through our Lord Jesus Christ.*
(1 Corinthians 15:54-57)

Death no longer has a hold on Christ or His people. The moment Christ died and rose, He won. Why? Because through His sacrifice, the price was paid. Our sins were forgiven. Our souls were bought by the precious blood of the Lamb. Christ was not defeated when He died, because He rose again. Our debts were paid when He died, and that is good news. That is the gospel. And that is the blessed atonement that we receive through Christ crucified.

BECAUSE OF CHRIST CRUCIFIED, WE RECEIVE OUR ABOLITION

*Grace to you and peace from God our Father and
the Lord Jesus Christ, who gave himself for our sins
to deliver us from the present evil age, according to
the will of our God and Father, to whom be the glory
forever and ever. Amen.* (Galatians 1:3-5)

The reason Jesus *gave himself for our sins* was *to deliver us from the present evil age.* There is a power in this world that we cannot overcome apart from Christ. So Jesus came to set us free from that power of sin that binds us, because a power exists in this world that we cannot overcome apart from Christ.

Abolition is a term connected with the ending of slavery. And those who fight for the freedom of those enslaved are called abolitionists. Jesus Christ is our Great Abolitionist. Good Friday is a day of liberation and freedom. Another blessing we receive through Christ crucified is our freedom from slavery and sin. There is a power in this present age that binds us and blinds us that only Jesus can save us from.

Romans 6:22-23 states,

But now that you have been set free from sin and
have become slaves of God, the fruit you get leads to
sanctification and its end, eternal life. For the wages
of sin is death, but the free gift of God is eternal life
in Christ Jesus our Lord.

Faith in Jesus Christ, which is at the center of the gospel, is the only way people can truly be set free – free from sin, free from bondage, free in this life, and free for eternity.

A GOSPEL FOUNDATION FOR MINISTRY

This message of freedom gives us the gospel foundation upon which our ministry was grounded. Christ crucified gives us our assignment to declare the gospel of Jesus Christ. This gospel must be a verbal declaration of the life, death, and resurrection of Jesus. Faith comes from hearing, and as people hear the gospel, understand it, and put their faith in Him, they will be saved. However, our declaration of this good news is not only verbal, but it is a visible witness as well. Our faith must be expressed through our deeds, because faith without deeds is dead (James 2:17). And Jesus calls us to let our light shine before others so that they may see our good works and give glory to the Father in heaven (Matthew 5:16). So our assignment from Jesus to declare His gospel is expressed through our words and our works.

The gospel gives us our blessed atonement from sin. We rejoice in knowing that our sins have been forgiven by the grace of God. All sins can be washed away by the power of the blood of the Lamb. There is no sin too big because the power of the cross is even bigger. There is no shame too deep because, in Christ, we become clothed with His righteousness, *not having a righteousness of my own that comes from the law, but that which comes through faith in Christ, the righteousness from God that depends on faith* (Philippians 3:9). He gives us a new standing and a new status as children who are holy, righteous, and pure. This is the hope we offer to all those who have sinned and have been sinned against in the dark world of slavery and human trafficking. And it is an overflow of love and thanksgiving to Jesus that moves us into the streets to share this message of hope to a people walking in darkness.

Seeking to end human trafficking and bring freedom to those enslaved is one of the clearest pictures of the gospel. It is a physical representation of what happened to us spiritually. Christians were once in bondage to sin, and Christ came to set us free. There are millions who are in bondage physically whom God loves and whom God's heart breaks for. The physical bondage is a picture of the spiritual bondage that they (and we) share apart from Christ. Jesus came to set them free so that they might know Him and delight in His love. This is the driving force of this ministry. Jesus came to give us our assignment, our atonement, and our abolition. We have been commissioned by our Savior to be His light and to shine His light into a darkened world. This pursuit of justice is not only out of obedience to His Word, but also out of deep thankfulness for the work of salvation that Jesus freely gave to us through His sacrifice.

GROUP DISCUSSION QUESTIONS:

- What distinction do you think the author was making when he said that this kind of ministry is not just about social justice but also biblical justice? What's the difference?

- What is our assignment from Christ? What does that look like for your life today?

- Do you feel abolition is an appropriate picture of the gospel? Why or why not?

PRAYER GUIDE:

- Pray for the purity of the gospel to remain intact in the justice movement of our generation.

- Pray for the church to boldly and faithfully declare and demonstrate the gospel.

- Give thanks to God for the freedom that we received through the cross of Jesus Christ.

CHAPTER 3

A BIBLICAL FOUNDATION OF JUSTICE

*But let justice roll down like waters, and righteous-
ness like an ever-flowing stream.* (Amos 5:24)

More than three hundred thousand children
younger than age eighteen are trafficked to serve
in armed conflicts worldwide.[25]

"So enormous, so dreadful, so irremediable did the [slave] trade's wickedness appear that my own mind was completely made up for abolition. Let the consequences be what they would: I from this time determined that I would never rest until I had effected its abolition." (William Wilberforce)

The word *justice* has been bandied about a lot in the press in recent days. *Justice* was *Merriam-Webster's* word of the year in 2018. In the early months of the 2020 Covid pandemic, we saw huge crowds of protesters gathered in major cities across the United States who chanted slogans and held signs of outrage demanding racial equality and justice after the death of George Floyd. From immigration issues to gender inequality to gun violence, cries for justice can be heard on an almost daily basis.

---

25 "Major Forms of Trafficking in Persons" (June 4, 2008), *Archived Content: U.S. Department of State: https://tinyurl.com/2r68w6fn* (February 27, 2023).

The concept of justice is not limited to mature adults. Even as children, we are deeply ingrained with it. Fairness and justice are concepts that children fully grasp. If you have two young children and give one five cookies while giving the other child just one cookie, the child with one cookie will exclaim, "That's not fair!" Or if you tell one child she can play outside while the other one has to work on her homework, the child who is sent to her room to do homework will naturally complain, "But that's not fair!"

Children have an innate understanding of justice deep within their souls because our God is a God of justice, and we are all made in His image. In his book *Mere Christianity*, C. S. Lewis pointed out that all these notions of fairness and right and wrong ultimately point to a moral law and a moral lawgiver – God. Thus, notions of justice won't go away. But while we may have a general understanding of right and wrong from childhood, what is the biblical way of understanding justice? This is what we will look at in this chapter.

GOD'S DEFINITION OF JUSTICE

What is God's definition of justice? The word for justice in Hebrew is *mishpat* and occurs more than two hundred times in the Bible in its various forms. The most basic meaning is "to treat people well,"[26] but it also carries the meaning of giving people what is due them, be it protection or punishment.[27]

And the Greek word for justice is *dikaiosyne*. Depending on the context, it can be translated as either "righteousness" or "justice." Over three hundred *dik*-stemmed words are found in the Greek New Testament. Some of the words are translated as "just" or "justice," but in most cases, the words are translated as "right" or "righteous." So depending on the context, *dikaiosyne* can mean

---

26   Timothy Keller, *Generous Justice: How God's Grace Makes Us Just* (New York: Riverhead Books, 2010), 2.
27   Ibid., 3.

"just" or "right." In Matthew 5:6, Jesus says, *"Blessed are those who hunger and thirst for righteousness, for they shall be satisfied."* And in Matthew 5:10, He says, *"Blessed are those who are persecuted for righteousness' sake, for theirs is the kingdom of heaven."* In both of these cases, *dikaiosyne* was translated as "righteousness." There are some who translate this to be "justice" instead.

Righteousness is ultimately gained through faith in Jesus Christ, and it becomes a part of our new status in Him. Justice has to do with a social situation being made right, where the peace, *shalom*, of God reigns. So those who are made right in Christ live a life of love to our neighbors, and that will also include seeking justice for them.

In Matthew 25:31-46, Jesus says,

> *"When the Son of Man comes in his glory, and all the angels with him, then he will sit on his glorious throne. Before him will be gathered all the nations, and he will separate people one from another as a shepherd separates the sheep from the goats. And he will place the sheep on his right, but the goats on the left. Then the King will say to those on his right, 'Come, **you who are blessed** by my Father, inherit the kingdom prepared for you from the foundation of the world. For I was hungry and you gave me food, I was thirsty and you gave me drink, I was a stranger and you welcomed me, I was naked and you clothed me, I was sick and you visited me, I was in prison and you came to me.' Then the **righteous** will answer him, saying, 'Lord, when did we see you hungry and feed you, or thirsty and give you drink? And when did we see you a stranger and welcome you, or naked and clothe you? And when did we see you sick or in prison and visit you?' And the King*

*will answer them, 'Truly, I say to you, as you did it
to one of the least of these my brothers, you did it
to me.' Then he will say to those on his left, 'Depart
from me, you **cursed,** into the eternal fire prepared
for the devil and his angels. For I was hungry and
you gave me no food, I was thirsty and you gave me
no drink, I was a stranger and you did not welcome
me, naked and you did not clothe me, sick and in
prison and you did not visit me.' Then they also will
answer, saying, 'Lord, when did we see you hungry
or thirsty or a stranger or naked or sick or in prison,
and did not minister to you?' Then he will answer
them, saying, 'Truly, I say to you, as you did not do
it to one of the least of these, you did not do it to me.'
And these will go away into eternal punishment, but
the **righteous** into eternal life."* (emphasis added)

Jesus honors the righteous in Christ in this passage, remembering that we are truly righteous only through the blood of Jesus
Christ as we trust in Him. We will never gain right standing or
righteousness by our own merit or deeds. And those who are
made right in Christ on the inside show the fruit of righteousness and love on the outside. By our fruit all people will know
that we belong to Him. In Christ, those who are made right will
shine His light. When did we see You hungry and feed You?
When did we visit You in prison? When did we see You naked
and clothe You? These are all acts of light and love in the form
of justice, compassion, and mercy. Another way to see it is that
those who are truly made righteous through Christ will live a
life of righteousness (or justice) as a sign of new life in Christ.

So treating people rightly or righteously is the essence of
justice. It is right living in the context of community. Justice and
righteousness are closely linked throughout Scripture. They are

so essential to God's kingdom that Psalm 89:14 even tells us that righteousness and justice are the foundation of God's throne.

Another way to see justice is the right use of power. Gary Haugen, the founder of International Justice Mission (IJM), says, "[J]ustice occurs on earth when power and authority between people is exercised in conformity with God's standards of moral excellence."[28] Simplifying it even further, Tim Keller states, "Justice is care for the vulnerable."[29] When people use power and authority to protect, provide, bless, and love their neighbor, justice exists within a society. Thus Scripture often describes justice as caring for the vulnerable in our communities – the poor, the widow, the fatherless, and the foreigner.

A primary manifestation of justice is caring for the outcast and oppressed within society. And to care for them means to meet their deepest needs. Are they hungry? Feed them. Are they naked? Clothe them. Are they oppressed? Set them free. Are they fearful? Protect them in such a way as to relieve them of their fears. Are they lost? Share the gospel with them. When we care for the vulnerable in our communities, we are establishing justice in the eyes of God. To God, justice is caring for the poor. *"You shall not pervert the justice due to your poor in his lawsuit"* (Exodus 23:6). It is caring for the fatherless, the widow, and the sojourner.

> *"You shall not pervert the justice due to the sojourner or to the fatherless, or take a widow's garment in pledge."* (Deuteronomy 24:17)

> *"'Cursed be anyone who perverts the justice due to the sojourner, the fatherless, and the widow.' And all the people shall say, 'Amen.'"* (Deuteronomy 27:19)

---

28   Gary Haugen, *Good News About Injustice: A Witness of Courage in a Hurting World,* 10th ed. (Downers, IL: IVP Books, 2009), 85.

29   Keller, *Generous Justice,* 3.

And who were the fatherless, the widow, and the sojourner of their day? They were the most vulnerable people within their society. So we see that God places a high value on the poor and oppressed within our society. To God, if they are vulnerable, then they are valuable. And to protect them and provide for them is to establish justice in our land.

So if justice is the right use of power, then injustice would be an abuse of power, when power is not used in a way that matches the excellencies of God's morality. Injustice in society is "taking advantage of those who have little or no economic or social power."[30] Haugen says, "Injustice occurs when power is misused to take from others what God has given them, namely, their life, dignity, liberty, or the fruits of their love and labor."[31] It is about the strong abusing, taking advantage of, and preying on the weak. When people no longer care for the weak, the poor, and the vulnerable, injustice will spread like a plague throughout society.

Although I grew up in the church, I rarely heard anything about God's heart for justice. But as I began to study this topic, I saw this theme saturated throughout Scripture. So if you're like me, maybe you also thought justice wasn't that big of a deal to our Christian faith. Let's take a journey through Scripture to see just how passionate God's heart is for justice.

OUR GOD OF JUSTICE

OUR GOD IS A GOD OF JUSTICE

Our quest for justice begins with beholding the God of justice. Our pursuit of justice must begin with a pursuit of God, because a foundational attribute of God is that He is a God of justice. It is the core of His being and the essence of who He is. So in our study of justice, we begin with God. Justice is God's design.

---

30 Kevin DeYoung, *Don't Call It A Comeback: The Old Faith for a New Day* (Wheaton: Crossway, 2011), 156.

31 Haugen, *Good News About Injustice*, 86.

Justice is God's desire. Justice is God's passion that beats within His heart. Our mighty God is a God of justice.

> *Therefore the LORD waits to be gracious to you, and therefore he exalts himself to show mercy to you.* **For the LORD is a God of justice;** *blessed are all those who wait for him.* (Isaiah 30:18, emphasis added)

The overflow of all that God does is from the place of justice, for all His ways are just.

> *"The Rock, his work is perfect,* **for all his ways are justice.** *A God of faithfulness and without iniquity, just and upright is he."* (Deuteronomy 32:4, emphasis added)

To know the ways of the Lord is to know the justice of God. Scripture says that the great and the wise know this about our God – that He is just.

> *Then I said, "These are only the poor; they have no sense;* **for they do not know the way of the LORD, the justice of their God.** *I will go to the great and will speak to them,* **for they know the way of the LORD, the justice of their God."** (Jeremiah 5:4-5, emphasis added)

JUSTICE COMES FROM THE LORD

Our hearts cry out for justice. So where do we turn? We turn to God, because God is the ultimate source of all justice. Every form of government we have seen throughout human history has proven that no one leader or type of government can truly establish justice in all the earth. The ultimate solution to the problem of injustice is found in Christ.

> *Many seek the face of a ruler, but it is from the*
> *LORD that a man gets justice.* (Proverbs 29:26)

God gives wisdom so that justice might be done. When just decisions are made, it is God who has blessed that person with the wisdom to make the right choice so that justice might be established within our land.

> *And all Israel heard of the judgment that the king*
> *had rendered, and they stood in awe of the king,*
> *because they perceived that the wisdom of God was*
> *in him to do justice.* (1 Kings 3:28)

In speaking of the coming Messiah, the Lord Jesus is the One through whom justice will finally be established over all the earth.

> *Behold my servant, whom I uphold, my chosen, in*
> *whom my soul delights; I have put my Spirit upon*
> *him; he will bring forth justice to the nations. He will*
> *not cry aloud or lift up his voice, or make it heard*
> *in the street; a bruised reed he will not break, and a*
> *faintly burning wick he will not quench; he will faith-*
> *fully bring forth justice. He will not grow faint or be*
> *discouraged till he has established justice in the earth;*
> *and the coastlands wait for his law.* (Isaiah 42:1-4)

> *In those days and at that time I will cause a righteous*
> *Branch to spring up for David, and he shall execute*
> *justice and righteousness in the land.* (Jeremiah 33:15)

GOD'S THRONE IS ONE OF JUSTICE

A throne is the symbol of power and authority. It represents the place where kings rule, where decisions are made, and where laws are enforced. Justice and righteousness are the foundation of His throne. His whole leadership and kingship flow from this foundation. It is from the place of justice that His kingdom is established.

> *Righteousness and justice are the foundation of your throne; steadfast love and faithfulness go before you.* (Psalm 89:14)

> *The LORD reigns, let the earth rejoice; let the many coastlands be glad! Clouds and thick darkness are all around him; righteousness and justice are the foundation of his throne.* (Psalm 97:1-2)

GOD'S DELIGHT IN JUSTICE

GOD LOVES JUSTICE

God not only rules in justice, but He also loves justice. It is the delight of His heart. And as people made in the image of God, we need to remember that our deep passion for justice is a small reflection of what is burning inside God's heart.

> *For the LORD loves justice; he will not forsake his saints. They are preserved forever, but the children of the wicked shall be cut off.* (Psalm 37:28)

> *"But let him who boasts boast in this, that he understands and knows me, that I am the LORD who practices steadfast love, justice, and righteousness in the earth. For in these things I delight, declares the LORD."* (Jeremiah 9:24)

GOD BLESSES JUSTICE

Another way Scripture reveals how much God delights in justice is the way it speaks of the blessings that belong to those who do justice. Blessings await those who help the oppressed and the poor. God will deal well with the one who pursues justice.

> Blessed are they who observe justice, who do righteousness at all times! (Psalm 106:3)

> It is well with the man who deals generously and lends; who conducts his affairs with justice. (Psalm 112:5)

> Blessed is he whose help is the God of Jacob, whose hope is in the LORD his God, who made heaven and earth, the sea, and all that is in them, who keeps faith forever; who executes justice for the oppressed, who gives food to the hungry. The LORD sets the prisoners free. (Psalm 146:5-7)

When a leader rules with justice, blessings of light and life flow to the people.

> The God of Israel has spoken; the Rock of Israel has said to me: When one rules justly over men, ruling in the fear of God, he dawns on them like the morning light, like the sun shining forth on a cloudless morning, like rain that makes grass to sprout from the earth. (2 Samuel 23:3-4)

GOD IN SCRIPTURE HONORS JUSTICE

David, who ruled as king over Israel, is remembered as being a man after God's own heart. In spite of his sins and failures, Scripture also remembers him as one who ruled with justice and equity.

> *So David reigned over all Israel. And David*
> *administered justice and equity to all his people.*
> (2 Samuel 8:15)

GOD'S DESIRE TO SEEK JUSTICE

JUSTICE IS COMMANDED TO HIS PEOPLE

The desire of God's heart is for His people to display His glory and His goodness upon the earth. One of the primary ways communities experience the blessings of safety, love, and goodness is when justice rules the land. For this reason, God commands His people to do justice and to hold on to it with all their might. We need to understand that "[j]ustice is the work of community. It cannot be pursued alone. Justice is a manifestation of Christ's body working at its very best."[32] God's desire is for justice to be overflowing into society as an ever-flowing stream, beginning with His people.

> *"So you, by the help of your God, return, hold fast to*
> *love and justice, and wait continually for your God."*
> (Hosea 12:6)

> *Hate evil, and love good, and establish justice in the*
> *gate; it may be that the LORD, the God of hosts, will*
> *be gracious to the remnant of Joseph.* (Amos 5:15)

> *He has told you, O man, what is good; and what*
> *does the LORD require of you but to do justice, and*

---

32   Bethany H. Hoang, *Deepening the Soul for Justice* (Downers Grove: InterVarsity Press, 2012), 24.

*to love kindness, and to walk humbly with your
God?* (Micah 6:8)

As we can see throughout Scripture, justice is heavy on God's
heart. We are to treat one another in a way that reflects God's
righteous character. It is right and righteous living in the context of community. It is an expression of loving our neighbor
as ourselves. This pursuit is biblical, and as we saw in the previous chapter, it is also grounded in the gospel of Jesus Christ.

GROUP DISCUSSION QUESTIONS:

- Which verses stood out to you the most and why?
  Did anything surprise you about what was said
  in Scripture about justice or how often Scripture
  spoke of it?

- Who would be considered a group in your community that is in need of help and compassion
  today? Make a list of people or groups who would
  be longing for support right now.

- Looking at that list, how many are being cared for
  by churches in your community? Is there something your group could do to love them or meet
  their needs?

PRAYER GUIDE:

- Ask God to open your eyes to those in need in your community with His eyes of love and compassion.

- Pray for those who are vulnerable in your community. Pray that they will be protected and cared for and know the love of Jesus.

- Pray for your church and the churches in your community to be active in sharing the love of Jesus in tangible ways to those who are in need.

CHAPTER 4

THE KINGDOM VALUE OF VULNERABILITY

"Give justice to the weak and the fatherless; maintain the right of the afflicted and the destitute. Rescue the weak and the needy; deliver them from the hand of the wicked." (Psalm 82:3-4)

Children account for half of the victims of human trafficking.[33]

K eller reminds us that "God personally identifies very closely with the widow, the orphan, and the immigrant, the most powerless and vulnerable members of society."[34]

It's fascinating to see how, when you love someone, you notice and are drawn to the things they like. My wife's favorite flowers are freesia, so I keep an eye out for them whenever I see them. Because freesia is not commonly found, I make sure to get some for her whenever I find them. I never cared about flowers before, and I never looked for freesia before, but now I do because I love her.

This is also true for my son, Enoch. He was obsessed with

---

33   "How You Can Help the District Combat Human Trafficking," *Human Trafficking Fact Sheet. Office of the Attorney General for the District of Columbia: https:// tinyurl.com/4kabws3b* (March 2, 2023).

34   Keller, *Generous Justice*, 185.

Hot Wheels cars for the majority of his childhood (between the ages of two and nine). He would have one in his hand at all times, whether he was eating, bathing, or sleeping. So whenever I traveled or went shopping, I kept an eye out for them (thankfully, they were only about a dollar each). I had never noticed these small cars in stores before, but because I loved my son and knew he loved them, I started noticing them everywhere. And I enjoyed buying these cars for him because I adore him. When you truly love someone, you notice, and even love, the things they love.

This is true with our love relationship with God. Those who love God notice and love the things that God loves. So what does God love? We will explore in this chapter how the vulnerable hold a special place in God's heart.

THE VULNERABLE ARE A PRIORITY FOR GOD'S KINGDOM

The foundation of a building is its most important part. The foundation of a kingdom represents the core values on which it rules. What does Scripture reveal to be the foundation of God's kingdom? Psalm 89:14 tells us. *Righteousness and justice are the foundation of your throne; steadfast love and faithfulness go before you.* Righteousness and justice are the foundation of the kingdom of God, pointing us to the kind of kingdom that Jesus Christ would come to establish. They are the two key pillars on which His reign and rule are governed. So then why are righteousness and justice so vital to the kingdom?

Righteousness is about right living within our hearts, and justice is about right living with our neighbors. Righteousness is where we begin. Our ability to become righteous was accomplished through the sacrificial death of Jesus Christ on the cross, and that was an expression of love towards us. *For our sake he made him to be sin who knew no sin, so that in him we might become the righteousness of God* (2 Corinthians 5:21). This first pillar of God's kingdom is about the righteousness that is at the core of God's being, which is also the nature that is given to all who trust in Christ. His righteousness becomes our righteousness. That right living and right standing within our hearts before a holy God is a gift of grace that is received through faith in Jesus.

Justice is right living with our neighbors and in our communities. Justice is loving our neighbors as ourselves. It is love in action. It is more than just loving our family or those who are most like us; it extends beyond those with whom we are most comfortable. True neighbor love, true justice, involves caring for the vulnerable, the weak, the poor, and the oppressed.

These two things, righteousness and justice, are the foundation of God's throne. A throne symbolizes a king's power, authority, and rule over his kingdom. So justice and righteousness are foundational to the kingdom that we are a part of as believers. Foundations are pivotal, and they are a priority. All other things are built on top of the foundation. That is why as the true source of righteousness and justice, Jesus Christ is the foundation and cornerstone for the church in the New Testament (1 Corinthians 3:11; Ephesians 2:20). Our lives, the church, and the kingdom of God are all built from the foundation of Jesus Christ.

Quoting Isaiah 61, Jesus declares at the start of His public ministry:

> *"The Spirit of the Lord is upon me, because he has anointed me to proclaim good news to the poor. He has sent me to proclaim liberty to the captives and recovering of sight to the blind, to set at liberty those who are oppressed, to proclaim the year of the Lord's favor."* (Luke 4:18-19)

Jesus says His ministry will declare the good news of the gospel to the lost and demonstrate the good news of the gospel to the poor and oppressed. Justice is an expression of the gospel, and the gospel is the solution for injustice! Jesus continues to stress the priority this has for the spiritual leaders of His day:

> *"Woe to you, scribes and Pharisees, hypocrites! For you tithe mint and dill and cumin, and have neglected the **weightier** matters of the law: **justice and mercy and faithfulness.** These you ought to have done, without neglecting the others."*
> (Matthew 23:23, emphasis added)

So the religious leaders were careful to tithe and sacrifice and worship, but Jesus says they overlooked something crucial. In fact, He rebukes the leaders for neglecting what He calls *the weightier matters.* What were these weightier matters? Justice. Mercy. Faithfulness. Belief. Faith in who Jesus was would have transformed how they saw the world and how they lived in the world. It would have changed how they treated their neighbors and how they treated those who were in need:

- Those who need food – the hungry
- Those who need a family – the orphan
- Those who need finances – the poor
- Those who need freedom – the oppressed
- Those who need shelter – the refugee

As you read throughout Scripture, you will quickly realize there are groups of people whom God seems to have a special eye towards. True citizens of God's kingdom put justice for the vulnerable as a priority within their lives. *He has told you, O man, what is good; and what does the* LORD *require of you but to do justice, and to love kindness, and to walk humbly with your God?* (Micah 6:8). A life of justice expressed in kindness and love is how kingdom citizens walk before God.

THE VULNERABLE ARE A PEOPLE PRECIOUS TO GOD'S HEART

Few people hold such a dear place in God's heart as the fatherless and the widow, and the weak and the needy.

Psalm 82:3-4 – *"Give justice to the weak and the fatherless; maintain the right of the afflicted and the destitute. Rescue the weak and the needy; deliver them from the hand of the wicked."*

Exodus 22:22 – *"You shall not mistreat any widow or fatherless child."*

Deuteronomy 10:18 – *"[God] executes justice for the fatherless and the widow."*

Deuteronomy 24:17 – *"You shall not pervert the justice due . . . to the fatherless, or take a widow's garment in pledge."*

Deuteronomy 24:19 – *"When you reap your harvest in your field and forget a sheaf in the field, you shall not go back to get it. It shall be for . . . the fatherless, and the widow."*

Psalm 146:9 – *The LORD . . . upholds the widow and the fatherless.*

Zechariah 7:10 – *"Do not oppress the widow, the fatherless, . . . or the poor."*

Who were the fatherless and the widows? They were the most vulnerable people in society. Money, land, houses, and ownership were all transferred down generations through the male lineage. Without a male heir, a household was left with little hope. That is why in the book of Ruth, when Naomi lost her husband and her sons, all seemed hopeless, and she called herself "bitter."

This reveals something utterly crucial for us to know about God and His kingdom:

- The deeply vulnerable are deeply valuable to the heart of God.

- The deeply vulnerable in society are deeply valuable in God's kingdom.

Caring for the rejected in this world will bring reward in the next. Do you realize that the poor, the orphans, the elderly, and the trafficked prisoners are the "MVPs" of heaven on earth? They are precious to the heart of God. This was a radical paradigm shift in my understanding of how we need to do outreach within our community.

In a parable Jesus said, *"'I was hungry and you gave me food, . . . I was naked and you clothed me, . . . as you did it to one of the least of these . . . you did it to me'"* (Matthew 25:35-40). So to care for the least in our world is to care for Jesus. Are you seeing the vital connection here? These are people who matter greatly to the heart of God.

This is what the Spirit is calling the church to do in this hour because, like the Pharisees, we have for far too long ignored the more important matters of God's heart. We have become too comfortable within the confines of a building, even as God calls His people to go out into the world.

I like how one pastor puts it. "There is a caste system in God's kingdom. But it's the exact opposite of how this world works. The world will applaud the wealthy, the powerful, the beautiful, the talented, but it's not how God's system works. The special ones in God's kingdom are the weak ones. The ones who can't fight for themselves, who can't speak for themselves, and who can't feed themselves.

"We are to treat these people as the royalty of heaven here on earth. For the way you treat them is how you're ultimately treating God. What you do to the least of these is how you're treating God. Christianity brings what has been purchased by the cross, the culture of heaven and the nature of Jesus Christ, and transplants that into the hearts of men and women here on earth. What we see here on earth is a reflection of God's kingdom here on earth."[35]

Eric Ludy is a pastor with a strong desire for justice. He researched the poverty and oppression of children in Liberia, and one night, God gave him a dream and woke him up at 2:00 a.m. God showed him a picture of a little four-year-old boy sitting on the side of the road in Liberia.

God asked him a question. "What if that little boy was your son?"

Eric replied, "My son? Hudson? What if my son was on the side of a dirt road, across the world from me, suffering? Totally alone? Not knowing what was happening, too young to understand what was going on in the world, abandoned with no one to fight for his cause and no one to help him find his way home? He'd be hungry, with no one there to feed him, starving and alone? What would I do if that was my son?!"

Eric answered God in this dream and said, "If there was a concrete wall between us in that situation, I would my claw my way through that wall with my bare hands! And if I couldn't get there, I'd call every friend I have and say, 'I have a son who

---

35 Taken from Eric Ludy's sermon excerpt "Depraved Indifference": *https://www. youtube.com/watch?v=UWHJ6-YhSYQ.*

is alone and needs help. I need you to get on a plane and get over there. I need you to just get to him and be a father to him, until I have him back in my arms.'"

God responded to him, "That child you see on the street, that's *My* Hudson, that's *My* child.

"That girl in the brothel in Seoul, that's *My* princess.

"That child in the orphanage, crying for someone to hold her, that's *My* baby.

"That twelve-year-old in the karaoke bar, that's *My* girl."

It is as though God is saying, "I am calling everyone who is called by My name, who calls themselves My friend, to go in My name and love them for Me!" God's Word tells us we are His body. Our hands are His hands to hold them and love them. Our feet are His feet to go where He would go. Our heart represents His heart to love them with His love.

We are the body of Christ. Many girls I have talked to over the years who have come out of sex trafficking (no matter their religious beliefs) have testified that at one point in their lives when things got really, really hard, they would cry out to God. They would say, "God, are you really there? If you're really there, then hear my cry for help! Hear my cry for freedom!" They cry out for God, and you and I are His body, called upon to show up and show them what God looks like. They are precious to God's heart.

THE VULNERABLE ARE THE PURSUIT OF GOD'S PEOPLE

There is a fascinating connection that Jeremiah makes with justice and the people of God.

Let us look at Jeremiah 22:15-16:

> "*Do you think you are a king because you compete in cedar? Did not your father eat and drink and **do justice and righteousness**? Then it was well with*

him. He judged the cause of the poor and needy;
then it was well. Is not this to know me? declares the
LORD.*"* (emphasis added)

God rebukes the king of Judah for neglecting justice and righteousness (the foundation of His throne). He says his father did these things; his father cared for the poor and needy, and things went well for them. Then God says, "Isn't this what it means to know Me?" He is saying that if we truly know Him, we will pursue justice and righteousness.

And in Jeremiah 9:23-24 it says,

Thus says the LORD: *"Let not the wise man boast*
in his wisdom, let not the mighty man boast in his
might, let not the rich man boast in his riches, **but**
let him who boasts boast in this, that he under-
stands and knows me, that I am the LORD **who**
practices steadfast love, justice, and righteousness
in the earth. *For in these things I delight, declares*
the LORD.*"* (emphasis added)

God says, "Don't boast if you have wisdom, and don't boast if you have money." Instead, He says, "If you only boast in one thing, and if you truly understand and know Me, then you know that I practice and pursue love, justice, and righteousness." For these are the things that God delights in! He loves justice and righteousness. These are the passions of His heart, and they become the passions of people who truly know their God!

God says, "If you know that I delight in love, justice, and righteousness, then you truly know Me. And now you can boast that you know Me." This is amazing. To know God is to know the passions of His heart. To pursue God is to pursue the passions of His heart. Therefore, those who pursue God will eventually pursue these values and foundations of the kingdom, such as love, justice, and righteousness in the earth.

We read in Isaiah that we are to *learn to do good; seek justice, correct oppression; bring justice to the fatherless, plead the widow's cause* (Isaiah 1:17). The word *seek* here means to "run after in hot pursuit of something." It would carry the idea of Pharaoh's army chasing after the Israelites in the desert as we read in Exodus.

When I was in second grade, my neighbor had a dog named Blackie. Blackie and I did not get along. The fence in our backyard kept us apart, so I would confidently mock him, blow in his face, and occasionally throw my baseball at the fence. Then one day, I was in the front yard of our house, and so was Blackie. And there was no fence between us. Our eyes locked on each other and Blackie was huffing and puffing. With no fence in his way and no leash on his neck, he knew he was free. So he ran after me with all his might, and I ran down the street for my life. I screamed and prayed for my deliverance, and by God's grace, I am alive today to tell you this story. But I share this traumatic piece of my childhood so you can get a picture of the kind of passionate pursuit God asks His people to have in pursuing justice in our world. God calls us to pursue justice for the oppressed and the vulnerable.

This verse in Isaiah also says to *learn to do good*. Many times we do not know what to do, and that is okay. That is why we are to learn what we can do. Learn what it means to seek after justice in our communities. Find out who the most vulnerable people are in your city or state. If the most vulnerable in our society are the ones that heaven takes special notice of, then take the time to find out who they are in your world.

While I was pastoring in Korea, we asked ourselves, "Who are the most vulnerable groups in our neighborhoods?" As a result, God led us to care for a number of groups: the homeless, the elderly, the refugees, stateless children, the trafficked, single moms, the orphan, and the unborn.

That may seem like a lot of ministries, but we were blessed with a lot of resources. We wanted to be faithful with the number of "talents" He entrusted to us, because to whom much is given, much is expected. If your resources are limited, then start with one group of people to focus on. Depending on your area, the vulnerable groups may look very different. We do not all have the same role to play, but we do have a role to play in the pursuit of justice in our generation.

GROUP DISCUSSION QUESTIONS:

- Prior to reading this chapter, why did you think the Bible so often speaks of caring for the orphan, the widow, and the fatherless?

- Do you agree with the statement that the deeply vulnerable are deeply valuable to the heart of God? Why or why not?

- Who would you say are the vulnerable groups in your community and city? What kind of ministry is being done or could be done to help them?

PRAYER GUIDE:

- Ask God to open the eyes of your heart and the heart of your church to see the vulnerable as valuably as God does.

- Pray for the church to love the vulnerable better and to find practical ways to be Christ to them.

- Ask God to give you His heart of compassion and passion for your neighbors.

CHAPTER 5

WHERE IS THE JUSTICE OF GOD?

The LORD works righteousness and justice for all who are oppressed. (Psalm 103:6)

Approximately 80 percent of trafficking victims are female, 50 percent are children, and 70 percent are used for sexual exploitation.[36]

Injustice occurs when power is misused to take from others what God has given them, namely, their life, dignity, liberty, or the fruits of their love and labor.[37]

THE PROBLEM IS INJUSTICE IN THE WORLD

It only takes one look at the evening news to see there is something very wrong in this world. A drunk driver crashes into another car and walks away healthy, while the driver in the other car will never walk again. The CEO of a large company is found guilty of stealing millions of dollars but only faces a three-month probationary term, while a homeless man steals a

---

36 Shelley, *Human Trafficking*, 5.
37 Haugen, *Good News About Injustice*, 85.

hundred dollars and is sentenced to over fifteen years in jail. A fourteen-year-old girl is forced into a car, but the police officer nearby does nothing except count the money he just received from the trafficker and puts the money into his shirt pocket, right behind his police badge.

There is great injustice in our world, but why? Why is there such evil surrounding us? There are many factors we can look at, but the Bible tells us the fundamental cause. We live in a fallen, sin-stained, and broken world. The reason for the great injustice in our world is because there is great unrighteousness within the human heart. The apostle Paul tells us that *"none is righteous, no, not one"* (Romans 3:10) and that *all have sinned and fall short of the glory of God* (Romans 3:23). The ultimate source of all injustice is the sin that lies within the heart of every person on this planet. The apostle Paul told Timothy that things will get even worse in the last days:

> *But understand this, that in the last days there will come times of difficulty. For people will be lovers of self, lovers of money, proud, arrogant, abusive, disobedient to their parents, ungrateful, unholy, heartless, unappeasable, slanderous, without self-control, brutal, not loving good, treacherous, reckless, swollen with conceit, lovers of pleasure rather than lovers of God. Indeed, all who desire to live a godly life in Christ Jesus will be persecuted, while evil people and impostors will go on **from bad to worse**, deceiving and being deceived.* (2 Timothy 3:1-4, 12-13, emphasis added)

There is something within the nature of sin such that if it is not dealt with properly, it grows. This is bad news.

Time and again we see our world filled with brokenness and injustice. We can relate to the psalmist who becomes envious of the arrogant when he sees the wicked prosper (Psalm 73:3). It is frustrating and infuriating to see those who do the evil get away with it. This creates a tension in our world that causes us to ask not only ourselves, but also the people in power: Can there be peace in our world if there is no justice?"[38] There is a restlessness in society until justice rules. When we look at the world around us, not only is there evil, but it also seems that evil people get away with their evil schemes! During every financial crisis, there are CEOs who walk away with million-dollar bonuses while millions of workers lose their jobs. That is a great injustice. Is there no one who notices? Is there no one who cares? Is there no one who can do something about these great injustices?

The answer to these cries for justice is a resounding YES! YES! There is someone who notices! YES! There is someone who cares! And YES! There is someone who will do something about it! Then what is the solution to this great problem of injustice in our world?

THE SOLUTION IS OUR GOD OF JUSTICE

God is the answer to the problem of injustice because God is the ultimate source of justice. *Therefore the LORD waits to be gracious to you, and therefore he exalts himself to show mercy to you. For the LORD is a God of justice; blessed are all those who wait for him* (Isaiah 30:18). This is a rich verse that exalts the grace and mercy of God in connection with the justice of God. God's solution to the injustice of man's rebellion is found in the grace of Jesus Christ that attained justice for all who would believe in Him through His death upon the cross. *Many seek the face of a ruler, but it is from the LORD that a man gets justice* (Proverbs 29:26). Justice may come through an earthly judge or

---

38   Alan E. Lewis, *Between Cross and Resurrection: A Theology of Holy Saturday* (Grand Rapids: William B. Eerdmans Publishing Company, 2001), 323.

a court system, but according to Scripture, the ultimate source of justice originates from God. God is the ultimate source of justice because He is the Judge over all the earth.

God is Judge and that is good news. So what does this mean? J. I. Packer reminds us of the significance of God's role as Judge.[39] We must remember that a judge is a person identified with what is good and right. To be a judge means this person has moral excellence to make the right decision. He is not biased or impartial. Another attribute of a judge is that this person has great wisdom and the ability to discern truth. Also, the judge is a person of power and has authority to execute the sentence. He is able to do something about the wrong that has been committed. That is our God! So we do not worry or grow weary, because our God is the good Judge over all the earth.

But if He is the Judge and is able to do something, why does injustice still exist? Does He not care? He does care. He has done something about it. He will do something about it. And He desires the church to do something about it. Now it's important for us to look at the ways in which God brings about justice in the world.

GOD'S SOLUTION FROM THE BEGINNING: THE CROSS

When we see injustice in this world, we need to see it through the lens of God's complete story of redemptive history. The scope of all of Scripture and the story that God is writing can be seen in these four movements: Creation. Fall. Redemption. Consummation. Ever since the fall (where sin and injustice entered our world), God had a plan, and that plan would be realized in the life, death, and resurrection of His Son, Jesus Christ. Therefore, Jesus is central in understanding where the justice of God can be found.

Let's begin by looking at what Jesus said at the start of His public ministry. Luke 4:16-19 says,

---

39   J. I. Packer, *Knowing God* (Downers Grove: IVP Books, 1973), 125 ff.

*And he came to Nazareth, where he had been
brought up. And as was his custom, he went to the
synagogue on the Sabbath day, and he stood up to
read. And the scroll of the prophet Isaiah was given
to him. He unrolled the scroll and found the place
where it was written, "The Spirit of the Lord is upon
me, because he has anointed me to proclaim good
news to the poor. He has sent me to proclaim liberty
to the captives and recovering of sight to the blind,
to set at liberty those who are oppressed, to proclaim
the year of the Lord's favor."*

Jesus came to declare good news to those who experienced bad
news in this fallen world. This good news was declared in expressing grace in various forms, including liberty, healing, and mercy.

People will quote these verses, especially the part of pro-
claiming liberty to the captives and setting the oppressed free,
as the basis for our fight against human trafficking. This is true,
but we must keep in mind that there is both a physical and a
spiritual element to justice. In the justice movement of our day
we are called upon to care for the physical needs of the poor, the
hurting, and the captives. That is justice. But we must not lose
sight of the fact that the primary mission of Jesus was to bring
spiritual freedom, *spiritual* healing, and a *spiritual* blessing to
all who were captives of sin. If someone is free physically but
never experiences spiritual freedom from sin, then that person
will still be bound to chains that can harm them forever in
eternity. Let us love people by seeking their freedom physically,
spiritually, and for eternity.

But a weakness of the evangelical church in recent history has
us concerned only about the spiritual freedom of the soul with no
vital concern about the physical condition of others. Thankfully,
we see changes in this mentality in the recent justice movement

that is beginning in our generation. We must realize that to truly love a person means to love their whole being – physical, spiritual, emotional, and mental. To be concerned only for the spiritual welfare of a person makes the person feel like they are a project to work on or win over instead of as a person to love.

What I have found time and again is that when we love people by caring for their physical needs, it opens their hearts to hear the gospel message for spiritual freedom as well. But we must never use caring for the physical needs of others only as our foot in the door to try to evangelize others. Let us be a generation that will truly love our neighbors in whatever way we can, whenever we have the opportunity. We must live out the gospel, not just say it. The gospel must be declared *and* demonstrated. It must be lived out in love as well as spoken of with truth.

Let us now look back at how this opening statement of Jesus is grounded in the spiritual freedom He came to bring. Returning to Luke 4, Jesus quotes Isaiah 61. Pastor Tim Keller points out an important omission here. What is interesting is the part that Jesus leaves out of His quoting Isaiah 61. He stops mid-sentence in verse 2 of the Isaiah passage.

He quotes this:

> *The Spirit of the Lord GOD is upon me, because the LORD has anointed me to bring good news to the poor; he has sent me to bind up the brokenhearted, to proclaim liberty to the captives, and the opening of the prison to those who are bound; to proclaim the year of the LORD's favor.* (Isaiah 61:1-2)

And then Jesus stops right there. Look at what He leaves out – *and the day of vengeance of our God; to comfort all who mourn.* Now why would He do that? Is He trying to soften up the mission and the message? Hardly. The reason Jesus leaves out the wrath of God at the start of His public ministry is because He is the one who will take the wrath of God at the end of His public ministry. I believe Jesus is saying, "I will not declare God's vengeance and wrath to you. Instead, I will take God's vengeance and wrath *for* you!"

The good news is that Jesus is the one who will absorb the wrath and vengeance of God on the cross, if we will only believe in Him. John 3:16-17 tells us:

> *"For God so loved the world, that he gave his only Son, that whoever believes in him should not perish but have eternal life. For God did not send his Son into the world to condemn the world, but in order that the world might be saved through him."*

Jesus came to take the vengeance, condemnation, and wrath of God that was intended for us! My injustice against a holy, just God was dealt with when Jesus took my penalty. God had a plan to deal with sin, evil, and injustice from the beginning, and the ultimate way He sought to deal with it was through the cross of Jesus Christ. John Stott says, "By bearing Himself in Christ the fearful penalty of our sins, God not only propitiated His wrath, ransomed us from slavery, justified us in His sight and reconciled us to Himself, but thereby also defended and demonstrated His own justice."[40]

Jesus' ministry was marked by a deep concern for the poor, the sick, and the oppressed in society. But before we start looking at the injustices of others, we need to look at the injustice in our own hearts. Remember that one of the greatest injustices of all is sin and rebellion against a holy God. It is to reject and dishonor Him. A penalty must be enforced, and a price must be paid because of this great injustice and offense. We were to

---

40   John Stott, *The Cross of Christ* (Downers Grove: IVP, 2006), 207.

receive that penalty, but Jesus took it for us. Jesus paid the price. He bore our punishment. He bailed us out. And Jesus bestowed upon us His righteousness as He places us in Him. This all happened when Jesus died on the cross for the sins of the world. God's solution for justice from the start was the cross of Jesus Christ. It is here that God rectified the great injustice of our rebellion through the death and resurrection of His only Son.

The great injustice of dishonoring God ends with the great justice of God receiving the worship due His name – for all who would put their trust in His name. This is the spiritual justice that changes lives for eternity and brings forth true freedom. It is the great act of grace that restores ultimate justice in the story of redemption.

All evil, injustice, and wrongs have been dealt with for those who trust in Jesus Christ. But what about those who will not place their faith and trust in Jesus Christ? Where is the justice for them? This leads us to another place where we find the justice of God.

GOD'S SOLUTION AT THE END: THE JUDGMENT

In Psalm 73, the psalmist wrestles with the question of injustice and seeing the wicked prosper, but he is comforted when he enters the *sanctuary of God* where he then understands their final destiny. For every evil, there is a day of justice coming. For every wrong done, for every injustice, there is a reckoning to face. It will be a day that will give each person what they truly deserve. Jesus speaks of this end-time judgment in John 5:22-29:

> *"For the Father judges no one, but has given all*
> *judgment to the Son, that all may honor the Son,*
> *just as they honor the Father. Whoever does not*
> *honor the Son does not honor the Father who sent*

him. Truly, truly, I say to you, whoever hears my
word and believes him who sent me has eternal life.
He does not come into judgment, but has passed
from death to life. Truly, truly, I say to you, an hour
is coming, and is now here, when the dead will hear
the voice of the Son of God, and those who hear will
live. For as the Father has life in himself, so he has
granted the Son also to have life in himself. And
he has given him authority to execute judgment,
because he is the Son of Man. Do not marvel at this,
for an hour is coming when all who are in the tombs
will hear his voice and come out, those who have
done good to the resurrection of life, and those who
have done evil to the resurrection of judgment."

The Gospels make it clear that those who have not believed in
the Son of God or trusted in Christ Jesus to save them from
their sins will face a day of great judgment. But those who
trust in Christ as the only way to be saved from their sins will
experience a day of resurrection unto life!

We see this in Revelation 20:13-15:

And the sea gave up the dead who were in it, Death
and Hades gave up the dead who were in them, and
they were judged, each one of them, according to what
they had done. Then Death and Hades were thrown
into the lake of fire. This is the second death, the lake
of fire. And if anyone's name was not found written in
the book of life, he was thrown into the lake of fire.

Every person who has not surrendered their lives and sins to
Jesus will face eternal judgment and damnation in the lake
of fire forever. Every pimp who has profited from the sexual

abuse of his captors, every trafficker who has destroyed the innocence of his victims, every customer who has stolen the sacred touch of intimacy from his victim, every person who has caused injustice to the least of these will face the full fury of God's wrath that has been storing up for generations! This wrath will bring forth justice for all of eternity.

Does God care? Oh, He cares! He weeps with His daughters who are weeping behind closed doors. He is angry at the treatment of His little girls, and He *will* demand justice to be served one day! That is why we cry out, "*Maranatha,* Our Lord, come!" That is the cry of God's people who face injustice all the day long. This is why we pray for His return – in order to see justice fully established on the earth. On the final judgment day, all evil, injustice, and sins will be dealt with for all who have not trusted in Jesus as Lord, Savior, and King. God will right all wrongs. Every sinner will get their just punishment. Every trafficker and pimp and john will get their due.

And we need faith in our God of justice to believe that He will deal with everyone the right way and in the right time. In the mighty faith chapter of Hebrews 11, faith was required and honored even in the act of establishing justice. I never noticed that justice was in this chapter before, but the connection is clear – it took faith to pursue justice. It takes faith to believe that our God is committed to justice in all the nations of the earth. It took faith to believe that His purposes will prevail in the end. And it took faith for these men and women of the past to enforce justice when it seemed the world was against them. As the great hymn "This Is My Father's World" reminds us, "Though the wrong seems oft so strong, God is the ruler yet."

*[W]ho through faith conquered kingdoms, **enforced justice**, obtained promises, stopped the mouths of lions* (Hebrews 11:33, emphasis added). It took faith to obey what God had called these men and women to do in the plight for justice.

So does this mean we just wait and see who will trust God and who won't? Are the cross and the last judgment the only places and times where we find God's justice? No. There is more.

God invites us to partner with Him in pursuing justice for the needy in our world today. Keller reminds us that "while clearly Jesus was preaching the good news to all, he showed throughout his ministry the particular interest in the poor and the downtrodden that God has always had."[41] So then what about today? What is the role of the church today? And what is the connection with the cross, final judgment, and today's actions for justice? Do we just do nothing because all will work out in the end?

GOD'S SOLUTION FOR TODAY: THE CHURCH

Our justice movement must flow from two realities of God's justice: the cross and the final judgment. If it does not keep one eye on the cross and one eye on eternal judgment in the end, then our movement will become a humanistic, self-righteous act, rather than a biblical, gospel-centered one. If we don't look at the cross, we will think that the sins of the traffickers are worse than our sins, and we can become arrogant, judgmental, and self-righteous. The danger is to think that we are somehow better than they are, and that we are the solution to the world's problems. If we don't look at the final judgment, we will become frustrated seeing all this evil around us. We will think that God is not fair or just.

So where is the justice of God? There are three places where we find God's justice: at the cross, at the judgment, and in the church. God's justice was initiated with the cross, and it will be completed on judgment day. But justice must be sought out, expressed, and established in faith and in love today. There is an *already/not yet* tension in which we are living with the coming of God's kingdom

---

41   Keller, *Generous Justice*, 44.

and the kingdom that is here. "Although the kingdom is here in the finished work of Christ, the ministry of the Holy Spirit, and the witness of the church, this presence is partial and mysterious, for the kingdom is yet to be consummated. There remains a future eschatological aspect to the kingdom. Biblical theologians often say that the kingdom has been inaugurated, but is yet to be consummated, or that the kingdom is both already and not yet."[42]

The part of God's kingdom that is already here, through the church, must advance and show what the kingdom of God looks like as we walk in faith, hope, and love.

Before we even think about dealing with the injustices of others, we need to deal with the injustice that we have done before God. Our first response towards injustice is to look to God in faith. It begins with faith in Christ for the forgiveness of our sins and evils that we have committed throughout our lives. Yes, there are great evils within this world that we must fight, but before we look at the speck of sawdust in our brother's eye, Jesus tells us to first take the log out of our own eye. If we take an honest examination of our heart, we will find that there is great evil that lives within our lives as well. We need to kill it and surrender it at the feet of Jesus. We are sinners who have committed great injustices, and we can only be freed and restored through faith in Christ.

Secondly, our response towards those who do injustice is to pray that they will put their hope in God. First Timothy 6:10 tells us that *the love of money is a root of all kinds of evils.* That pretty much sums up the motive of trafficking at its core – greed. So after telling us how the love of money is a root of all kinds of evils, Paul then encourages Timothy to tell the churches:

> *As for the rich in this present age, charge them*
> *not to be haughty, nor to set their hopes on the*

---

42   Michael D. Williams, *Far as the Curse is Found: The Covenant Story of Redemption* (Phillipsburg, NJ: P&R Publishing, 2005), 269.

uncertainty of riches, but on God, who richly pro-
vides us with everything to enjoy. (1 Timothy 6:17)

Preaching the gospel is one way that freedom is experienced for those who are spiritually enslaved. We must pray that every trafficker and pimp would be set free from the bondage of greed, lust, and immorality that enslaves them, and instead, put their hope in Christ. Our desire is for society to bring them to justice, but we also pray that they would be healed and restored from the things that bind them. As we keep our eyes on the cross and on the day of judgment, we seek to bring these people into a saving knowledge of Jesus so that their lives can be transformed by the gospel and that they will experience grace and justice through the cross of Jesus.

Julie, one of our HOPE Be Restored (HBR) members, shared this testimony from a young woman who found rescue in a Christian-based restoration center in the United States. Her father, a drug addict, sold his own daughter – just a child – for money. He allowed her to be raped for as many times a day as it took to supply his habit.

The girl told Julie, "Day after day, men would come and go for their thrill of violating and abusing me in my childish state. Some would just fulfill their fantasies and walk out of the bedroom. They often seemed bemused by their actions. But one day, after violating me for money, a man broke down in tears at the foot of my bed and bawled, 'Why do I keep doing this to you?'"

Incredibly, years later after she had found Jesus as her Savior, she was able to accomplish something astounding. She forgave the men who had taken advantage of her. And she even forgave her father. She told her story with utter freedom and compassion for her abusers. This can only come from the power of Christ.

This flies in the face of how the world thinks of justice and mercy. But healing – true, deep, and profound healing – came from Christ, enabling her to find the freedom to forgive. Julie said, "This is one of the testimonies heard from a woman who has been truly freed of her chains knowing that her Father was her saving grace. Her forgiveness of her abusers and her own father were a very strong testimony of the ultimate importance the Lord's gospel plays in true freedom."

A third response for the church is to love the victims of injustice. This justice movement must be driven by love. It is motivated out of our love for God and our love for our neighbor. Therefore we must feed the poor, we must clothe the naked, and we must fight for the trafficked victim. Love, mercy, generosity – that is justice to God. You see, justice in God's kingdom is not just about upholding the law, but also about caring for the vulnerable and the broken in our communities. This justice movement is one of the greatest ways to show love to our neighbors.

We are to love both the victims and the perpetrators. God will call some to focus their ministry efforts on those who have been trafficked, but God will also call others to focus their time on serving those who do the trafficking. Both require supernatural, unconditional love.

After Jesus said that loving God and loving our neighbors was the mark of true life, a lawyer asked Him, "Who is my neighbor?" meaning, Whom don't I have to love? Jesus then tells the parable of the good Samaritan and ends with this in Luke 10:36-37:

> "Which of these three, do you think, proved to be a
> neighbor to the man who fell among the robbers?"
> He said, "The one who showed him mercy." And
> Jesus said to him, "You go, and do likewise."

So who is the one who lived a life of proper love and justice? The one who showed mercy, love, and generosity to those in need.

As it says in the book of Micah:

*He has shown you, O mortal, what is good. And
what does the* LORD *require of you? To act justly and
to love mercy and to walk humbly with your God.*
(Micah 6:8 NIV)

Where is justice? The world is meant to see it – in you!

GROUP DISCUSSION QUESTIONS:

- Why is it important to begin our justice movement
  by looking to the cross of Jesus? Why should we
  examine our own injustice towards God first?

- How do you feel about the final day of judgment?
  Will it be a day of hope or of dread? Explain.

- What is your current understanding of the church's
  role in seeking justice in our world?

PRAYER GUIDE:

- Thank God for the ways the cross of Jesus dealt
  with all the injustices of our sin.

- Pray for a deeper faith that trusts God to deal with
  all injustices in due time.

- Pray that your church will do its part in partnering with God and His gospel to bring forth justice
  in our generation.

CHAPTER 6

WHY THE CHURCH MUST LEAD

*He has told you, O man, what is good; and what
does the LORD require of you but to do justice,
and to love kindness, and to walk humbly with
your God?* (Micah 6:8)

Every year, nearly two million children are
exploited in the global commercial sex trade.[43]

Christ has no body now but yours, no hands, no
feet but yours. Yours are the eyes through which
He looks with compassion on this world; yours are
the feet with which He walks to do good; yours are
the hands with which He blesses all the world.[44]

A BUMP IN THE ROAD

Thanks to a contact, one day I was able to meet with an
official in the South Korean government to discuss the
issue of human trafficking and sex trafficking in his country.
He had the authority and power to make decisions, and he had

---

43   "Major Forms of Trafficking in Persons," (March 6, 2023).

44   Saint Teresa of Avila, "Christ Has No Body Now But Yours, *The Catholic
       Storeroom: https://tinyurl.com/2p836nhf* (March 6, 2023).

the ears of the highest levels of government. I was grateful that one of my colleagues was able to arrange an appointment with this high-ranking politician. I assumed that once he learned the shocking truth about this problem, he would be able to inform the appropriate people and perhaps something would be done.

To my surprise, he simply nodded and brushed past my presentation. Then, taking my arm and leading me away from the group, he spoke to me privately, as if it were "off the record."

"Why are you doing this?" he asked.

I was confused. Had he not just heard our discussion? Did we need a translator? Again, I went over the seriousness of human trafficking and the impact that it has.

"Yes, but why are you doing this? Don't you know that all men do this? Haven't you done this?"

I was astounded by his bluntness. He literally thought that human trafficking was not a serious problem. His message to me was, "You don't belong here. You shouldn't be doing this."

Later, when I discovered the real estate blueprints of one of Seoul's most infamous red-light districts, I discovered that the government owned the properties and leased them to some of the most powerful pimps and organized criminal gangs. I suppose I shouldn't have been surprised. This is how the world responds.

That, however, came from a worldly government. True, I had hopes that this powerful official would listen to me, but we're dealing with people and institutions that do not know God. What did surprise me was the reaction I got from fellow believers and even pastors. I expected rejection and misunderstanding from the world, but I didn't expect that same reaction from my church elders and other Christians who heard of our work.

In the weeks that followed, after I preached on biblical justice, I was excited to see the changes that happened in our church and the passion for God's justice that grew within the hearts of our congregation members. But as word spread about what our church was trying to do to end human trafficking, not everyone applauded our efforts. To my surprise, I got some strong emails that questioned our involvement in this movement.

"Are you turning into a social-gospel church?"

"I'm worried about you, Eddie. I don't like what I'm hearing about the direction you're taking your ministry."

I even received an email from someone who said, "I have to admit I have never heard any of your sermons, but based on what I'm hearing about your church, I know you're a social-gospel preacher." In short – you don't belong here.

The emails, criticisms, and attacks surprised me.

From the moment I first found out about the evil of human trafficking, I knew in my heart that the church needed to be involved. I never questioned or debated whether we, as a church, needed to embark on this journey toward justice.

Though it made sense in my head, I knew I needed to dig deeper into Scripture to ensure I could biblically defend our involvement in this justice movement. This was one of the driving forces behind the creation of this book. So, if you are a pastor or church leader reading this book in the hopes of starting a justice ministry in your own church, you will almost certainly face some opposition. You may wonder if pursuing freedom and justice is biblical. I hope that the previous chapters helped you see the heart of God through the lens of Scripture and acquire a strong conviction that pursuing justice is also an expression of the gospel. A justice ministry will not look the same for every church, but I believe every church is called to pursue justice. It may be through prayer, it may be through preaching, or it may be through a full-blown ministry, but every church has a role to play in living out the gospel in our world.

Here were the common objections I heard:

- It's not the church's role to be involved. Let the experts handle it. Stick to the gospel. Stick to ministry!

- It's just a passing fad. Stop chasing the latest trend.

- Isn't it too dangerous?

My responses were immediate. First, fighting for justice was an expression of the gospel. Didn't Jesus come to set the captives free? Don't these people who are trafficked and the traffickers need the visible and verbal presence of the church in their lives? My response to those who ask, "Shouldn't you just stick to ministry?" – This *is* ministry!

Second, this evil is so great, so systemic, so massive and entrenched that it's foolish to call it a passing fad or a trend. The slavery of today is worse than during the time of William Wilberforce, and it took him a lifetime to eradicate England's slave trade. This is no passing fad, and we should not have a sprinter's mentality. We need to be committed for the long haul.

And finally, yes, it is dangerous. After all, in some cities we are dealing with organized crime. During one trip to Thailand, a few of our team members and I went to a nearby convenience store to buy some ice cream after a long day of ministry. While we walked along a very deserted and dusty road back to our guesthouse, we saw a man down the road, twisting the arm of a lady. She tried to grab the keys to her scooter out of this man's hand, but he wouldn't give them back to her. She was clearly in pain. We took a few steps closer and realized that she was dressed like the women in the RLDs. The man was acting very much like her pimp. I wanted to help her, but I also calculated the risks. What if he had a gun or a knife? He was already very upset, so I didn't want to upset him further. But as I calculated our safety, Buri, one of our administrative staff members who was also our team member on that trip, nudged me on the arm and said, "Pastor Eddie! Do something!" So I looked around and saw that we were able to outnumber him. Also, JJ, one of our other team members, was a pretty big guy, so I decided to help the lady.

As I walked closer to him, I could feel my heart beating faster and faster. Thoughts of self-defense classes from my boyhood were quickly getting reviewed in my mind in case something were to happen. But right before I reached them, I said to JJ, "You got my back, right JJ?" No answer. "JJ?" I looked around, and all I saw was wide-eyed Buri silently clapping as I was about to confront this man. But looking further behind me, way across the street was JJ – who said he'd look after our other team members!

I had no time to turn around now. Here I was face-to-face with a man who was hurting and abusing a lady; she was clearly in need of help. So after taking a deep breath, I asked him, "Whose keys are those?" He stared long into my eyes and pointed his face towards the lady. So with my heart pounding so hard it felt like it was going to come out of my chest, I reached for the keys, took them out of his hands, gently gave them back to the lady, and said, "Then if these keys belong to her, we should give them back to her." He let go of her arm. I asked her if she was okay, and she nodded her head. She thanked me, started the engine of her scooter, and sped away. Thankfully, he also walked away, and I rejoined the rest of our team. Buri was so happy, but I was still catching my breath. When I realized what had just happened, I became extremely thankful for my safety.

We must be as wise as serpents in this battle. But if this were your son or daughter being violated, wouldn't you want the world to know about it and do something about it? There may be risks involved, but their lives are worth it. And true faith involves risk.

The church has become too accustomed to not taking risks. For far too long we've let governments and non-governmental organizations (NGOs) do what God has called the church to do.

We let others take the role of the church in our communities and forget that Jesus was the Great Abolitionist. In fact, we're letting the world take over our identity!

God calls the church to care for orphans, but we leave that to the agencies. God calls us to feed the poor, but we expect our government to take care of them. God calls us to care for the oppressed. God calls us to care for the vulnerable and we leave that to the NGOs. No, that is *our* job. It is what Jesus commanded.

Looking back, it was strange that I never once had to wonder if our church was supposed to be engaged in this fight for freedom for those enslaved in our world today. I never thought, *Does the church belong here?* It was a natural overflow after seeing what was happening, praying, and responding in obedience.

But that's an important question to ask. Does the church belong here? Does the church belong in this fight for the freedom of those enslaved by human traffickers? Are we in the right place? The answer is an emphatic yes!

And here's why.

THIS IS THE MISSION OF GOD

In this fight against the great evil of human trafficking in our day, it is my firm conviction that the church must not just be involved, but must also lead the way in the pursuit of freedom and justice. Why do I say this? Because true freedom and justice can only come through the gospel of Jesus Christ. Freedom and justice is why Jesus Christ came to this earth. He came to bring forth ultimate freedom from sin and to establish ultimate justice through His death upon the cross.

> *But thanks be to God, that you who were once slaves*
> *of sin have become obedient from the heart to the*
> *standard of teaching to which you were committed,*

and, having been set free from sin, have become
slaves of righteousness. (Romans 6:17-18)

The mission of Jesus was to die on the cross and be our atoning sacrifice so that we might be set free from sin. The problem that has affected all people is the problem of sin. As we saw in the last chapter, the injustice of human trafficking is, at its core, a sin problem, not an economic problem.

I was heading to speak at a conference in Asia when I struck up a conversation with a person who was sitting next to me. She asked where I was headed, and I told her about the human-trafficking conference I was attending. She was surprised that slavery still existed but suddenly paused and said, "I bet it's because of poverty that this happens. If people weren't poor, then this wouldn't happen." Her answer matched many other people's voices I've heard on this journey: It's because of poverty.

Does poverty alone really account for why the evil of human trafficking exists? Even if being poor was the sole factor, then Jesus has something to say to the poor too:

> *"The Spirit of the Lord is upon me, because he has*
> *anointed me to proclaim good news to the poor."*
> (Luke 4:18)

The good news for the poor is that even though you have nothing in this world, you can be rich in Christ. The good news for the poor is that wealth in this world is not the currency of true riches in heaven. Consider the testimony of one young woman, still a teenager, who found that she had no choice but to sell her body for money. The path to that nightmare life began not just with family dysfunction or poverty, but also with evil. This is what she told us:

Violated at the tender age of six, she was out on the street, trying to fend for herself by the age of twelve. Traffickers picked her up and forced her to be with men ten to twelve times a night. She said, "I thought I had to do it because my pimps told me to, but the more I did it, the more I felt dirty. I showered after it was over, and when I looked at myself in the mirror, I felt dirty. I scrubbed myself until my skin peeled off and bled, but I couldn't feel clean."

Other women we interviewed told us they had been beaten; some were held at knifepoint, and others were frequently choked nearly to death. But what hurt them the most? One rescued woman told us very calmly in a quiet but firm voice, "Listening to someone telling me that I was a whore; hearing things such as 'You are nothing!' 'I bought you; you belong to me.'" She paused. "That hurt me the most."

Another woman echoed this sentiment in our interview with her: "Sometimes I didn't feel like a human. We are not some objects you can buy with money. I wish [the johns] would at least treat us women as humans."

The deeper root of human slavery today is sin. And the reason Jesus came to this earth was to deal with the sin problem within every human heart. Jesus became the sacrificial Lamb who would pay the penalty for our sins and set us free from the power of sin that controls our lives. A major part of God's mission was to set us free from the bondage of sin. Another way of saying this is that "Jesus came to set the captives free!" This is our message. This is our mission.

What are the real issues we are up against when it comes to human trafficking and modern-day slavery? It is a heart issue. It is a moral issue. It is a spiritual issue at its core.

- The lust of the johns

- The greed of the traffickers

- The self-hatred and shame of the victims

- The hopelessness of the imprisoned

- The suffering of all who are still on the road to recovery

Everyone is in bondage concerning this issue, and only Christ can set us free. Only Jesus can restore hope and bring forth new life. The church has the only message that can set them free, not just physically but also spiritually and for eternity. It is a declaration of the gospel message that will bring true freedom, for Jesus Christ is the Great Abolitionist.

Jesus says, *"You are the salt of the earth"* and *"You are the light of the world,"* meaning you are change agents for society (Matthew 5:13-14). Where there is darkness, you are to shine and provide light and warmth. You shine light so that people can find the way, and so they can find warmth in the form of love to those who have lived in the cold of darkness for too long.

One day, members of our praise team visited Durebang ("My Sister's Home"), a shelter for migrant women of sex trafficking in the nearby city of Pyeongtaek. One of the women there was a Filipina worker in her late twenties who wore dark sunglasses, even indoors. She told the praise team her story, recounting how she had been lured into a job here and then tricked into an establishment that served as a cover for prostitution. Like so many others, many women from Southeast Asia come to South Korea under entertainment visas with promises to work in legitimate bars or restaurants, only to find themselves exploited and coerced into the sex trade.

When the praise team began leading a small service for the aftercare workers and survivors, the woman enthusiastically followed along in English, even though she wasn't familiar with any of the songs. Suddenly, in the midst of singing, she started to cry. The tears rolled down her face from behind her dark sunglasses. All her longing and her pain from the past few years spilled out. She was so happy to sing to the God who set her free – in every area of her life. The team returned to church deeply moved. They were reminded again of the joy that comes through the cross.

You see, the mission God gives us is to both declare and demonstrate the gospel through our lives. Jesus shows us what neighborly love is supposed to look like. He is a picture of a human being fully alive. Through His life we see that meeting the needs of the poor, the weak, the marginalized, and the oppressed is a demonstration of the visible gospel. He showed them in action that there is a God who loves them.

There was one fire station that had as its mission: "To save lives, property, and resources." And during 9/11, when lives needed saving, everyone ran away from the Twin Towers except the firefighters. Why? Their mission was to save lives, and part of fulfilling that mission sometimes required them to head into some dangerous situations. Our mission as the church is also to save lives. For some of us, it will mean we need to go to some difficult places. And if we're going to finish the mission Jesus gave us, it means going to places that are really dark and ugly because those are the places that are in desperate need of the gospel.

THIS IS THE VOICE OF GOD

I often hear people say how important it is to be a voice for the voiceless in this movement for freedom. I completely understand what they mean and where they are coming from, and I agree. Proverbs 31:8-9 even says, *Speak up for those who cannot speak for themselves, for the rights of all who are destitute. Speak up and judge fairly; defend the rights of the poor and needy* (NIV). Since the voice of the prisoners is not being heard, we must echo their cries for help and their demands for justice.

But as believers, I believe our higher responsibility is not just to be a voice for the voiceless; it is also to be the voice of God to the world. We are in this battle not just to answer the cry of the victim but also to answer the cry of God's heart to see justice roll down like a mighty river (Amos 5:24). Our voice must represent the voice of God to our world!

God's voice declares:

> *Give justice to the weak and the fatherless; maintain*
> *the right of the afflicted and the destitute. Rescue the*
> *weak and the needy; deliver them from the hand of*
> *the wicked.* (Psalm 82:3-4)

This voice must be heard in the church today. But we become His voice also for the victims of trafficking. They need to hear from God as we say to them:

- You are precious.

- You are beautiful.

- You are not trash.

- You are not forgotten.

The police will not say this to them. The government will not say this. The church must speak God's truth into their lives – truth that can set hearts free.

THIS IS THE IMAGE OF GOD

Another key reason the church must lead is that the fight for justice shows the world what God looks like.

> *Blessed is he whose help is the God of Jacob, whose*
> *hope is in the LORD his God, who made heaven and*
> *earth, the sea, and all that is in them, who keeps*
> *faith forever; who executes justice for the oppressed,*
> *who gives food to the hungry. The LORD sets the*
> *prisoners free; the LORD opens the eyes of the blind.*
> *The LORD lifts up those who are bowed down; the*
> *LORD loves the righteous. The LORD watches over*
> *the sojourners; he upholds the widow and the*

fatherless, but the way of the wicked he brings to
ruin. (Psalm 146:5-9)

This is a portrait of our God. So when we seek justice, show mercy, give generously, and extend kindness, what we are doing is showing people what our God looks like.

For the LORD *your God is God of gods and Lord of*
lords, the great, the mighty, and the awesome God,
who is not partial and takes no bribe. He exe-
cutes justice for the fatherless and the widow, and
loves the sojourner, giving him food and clothing.
(Deuteronomy 10:17-18)

Tim Keller, in his book *Generous Justice,* mentions how when he is a guest speaker somewhere, people will often ask him how he would like to be introduced. It is in that short introductory period that he needs to select the primary things he wants to be known for. He may teach at a seminary, but it's not the main thing he does. He's a pastor. It's the main title on his business card.

What about God's business card? How would He be introduced as a guest speaker? One of the primary things that God does in this world is to care for the poor and oppressed. The heart of God has always loved the poor, the orphan, and the widow. Moreover, many of these people are shuttled between international borders. They are forced to migrate and are stranded in strange lands against their will. They are the modern sojourners of today – the very same weary, frightened strangers whom God commanded us in Scripture to protect and care for.

The LORD *works righteousness and justice for all*
who are oppressed. (Psalm 103:6)

*"Cursed be anyone who perverts the justice due to
the sojourner, the fatherless, and the widow.' And all
the people shall say, 'Amen.'"* (Deuteronomy 27:19)

*Learn to do good; seek justice, correct oppression;
bring justice to the fatherless, plead the widow's
cause.* (Isaiah 1:17)

He cares for the least of these. Doing the good work of God
shows others the goodness of God in us. As DeYoung says,
"When we approach the world with a posture of love and generosity, our good works provide a powerful confirmation of
our declaration that 'God is love.'"[45]

*"Let your light shine before others, so that they may see your good
works and give glory to your Father who is in heaven"* (Matthew 5:16).
"You are the salt of the earth" (Matthew 5:13). Jesus calls us the
light of the world, and when He says that no one hides a lamp, it
means we don't stay away from dark places, we shine into them.

Trafficking today is one of the darkest evils in existence. It is
one of the most evil movements the world has ever seen. I believe
part of the reason it has become so enormous globally is that the
church has ignored it and avoided this dark evil far too long. It
is time for that to change. As people of light, we must find ways
to shine the light of God and the love of God into these places.

THIS IS THE MOVE OF GOD

*For everything there is a season, and a time for
every matter under heaven.* (Ecclesiastes 3:1)

For every season of injustice, God looks for people who will
respond to His call for justice. In his book *Issues Facing Christians*

---

45   DeYoung, Kevin, and Gilbert, Greg, *What is the Mission of the Church: Making
.   Sense of Social Justice, Shalom, and the Great Commission* (Wheaton: Crossway,
      2011), 225.

Today, John Stott reminds us that whenever God's people have been effective as salt and light in the community, there has been less social decay and more social uplift. In the United States, for example, after the early-nineteenth-century awakening associated with Charles G. Finney, born-again Christians were in the forefront of every major social reform in America. They spearheaded the abolitionist movement, the temperance movement, the peace movement, and the early feminist movement.[46]

John Wesley is best remembered for his preaching, through which he influenced the church to challenge and change society. He fought to stop the cruelty and torture of animals. He fought against the African slave trade. He fought against the kidnapping of fellow countrymen for their exportation and sale as slaves. He was a voice against gambling, prostitution, corruption, and many other evils and injustices of his day. Wesley was called both a preacher of the gospel and a prophet for social righteousness.

For William Wilberforce, we know him best for the ending of the transatlantic slave trade, but he was also a social reformer. He was nicknamed "the prime minister of a cabinet of philanthropists" and was at one time active in support of sixty-nine causes. He gave away 25 percent of his income to the poor. He fought for the rights of young boys to not have to work dangerous jobs in harmful conditions like chimney sweeping. He sought educational reform to provide all children with regular education in reading, personal hygiene, and religion. He fought to create agricultural reform to help provide affordable food for the poor. He influenced prison reform and the restriction of capital punishment from misuse and also helped support single moms, Sunday schools, and orphanages. He started groups like the Church Missionary Society, the British and Foreign Bible Society, and the Anti-Slavery Society.[47]

---

46 John Stott, *Issues Facing Christians Today* (Grand Rapids: Zondervan, 2006), 68.

47 "William Wilberforce," *Christian History, Christianity Today: https://tinyurl. com/mr3prvya* (March 6, 2023).

For the church, this is in our history. And we are in another season where God is calling forth His church to lead the way in justice and righteousness. We are in a special season of history for the ministry of the church. God is doing something globally on this issue. Thankfully, within the past decade, we have seen this issue rise up in widespread awareness.

In his book *The Meeting of the Waters,* Fritz Kling, after crossing the globe to see what the Spirit of God was doing in the churches around the world, listed his top seven findings in global trends. The number-one trend where he sees God moving through his churches is a movement towards mercy and social justice. He says,

"In the coming years, respect and relevance will flow to the global church when it does what it was created to do: to fill gaping holes, both spiritual and physical, in the lives of unnoticed, unwanted people. This is the heart language of the next generation, non-Christians and Christians alike, and it is the first global current – mercy."[48]

The speed at which this justice movement is growing is beyond human orchestration, and if the favor that God is giving to people involved in this movement is any indication, it reveals that this issue has been heavy on the Lord's heart for a long time. He has been waiting for His body to rise up and represent His love at this hour. The time is now for the church to step into this fight and move its way to the frontlines where we belong!

The Spirit is leading the church to declare and demonstrate the gospel to the darkest places in our cities, and we must respond with faith, obedience, courage, wisdom, humility, and love. "The greatest danger is that the valuable treasure carried by the church – the best news the world can ever hear – will be risked because leaders lack the stomach, mind, or heart to engage the changing times."[49]

---

48   Fritz Kling, *The Meeting of the Waters: 7 Global Currents That Will Propel the Future Church* (Colorado Springs: David C. Cook, March 1, 2010), 41.
49   Ibid., 27.

I do not want to leave these evils as an inheritance for our children's generation. I cannot just stand by and let the Enemy steal, kill, and destroy these precious children any longer. We must rise up in courage. We must rise up in prayer. We must rise up and be who God has called the church to be: the light of the world, shining in darkness, and a city on a hill that cannot be hidden.

GROUP DISCUSSION QUESTIONS:

- Define the gospel in your own words. How much of the gospel should be what we say versus what we do?

- Put into your own words why the church should be involved in this fight for justice.

- Do you believe the church should be leading this movement? Why or why not?

PRAYER GUIDE:

- Ask God to give you a greater understanding and appreciation of the gospel of Jesus Christ.

- Pray that the church will rise up and lead the way towards justice as we live out the gospel in our lives.

- Ask God to get you and your church on mission with Him.

CHAPTER 7

FREEDOM SUNDAY – PRACTICING SABBATH JUSTICE

"You shall remember that you were a slave in the land of Egypt, and the LORD your God brought you out from there with a mighty hand and an out-stretched arm." (Deuteronomy 5:15)

Thirty-one percent of victims (in the United States) in 2020 reported that their trafficker was a family member or caregiver.[50]

So there is also this aspect of Sabbath that is about justice, and it's this interplay of growing and practicing delight as a radical form of defiance against all forms of injustice, of a way of saying our humanity is meant for the glory of God.[51]

Sabbath celebrates the God who frees the heart from slavery.[52]

---

50   Elia Meltzer, "50+ Horrific Labor Trafficking Statistics and Examples," *Etactics* (July 21, 2022): *https://etactics.com/blog/labor-trafficking-statistics* (March 9, 2023).

51   The Allender Center, "Sabbath, Explained," *The Allender Center at the Seattle School* (February 5, 2021): *https://theallendercenter.org/2021/02/sabbath-explained/* (March 9, 2023).

52   Dan Allender, *Sabbath: The Ancient Practices* (Nashville: Thomas Nelson, 2009), 185.

Freedom Sunday is one way our church commemorated the freedom we have in Christ as well as remembering the freedom that millions in the world have yet to experience. On this weekend, we sing the praises of our great liberator, hear the Scripture's message of justice, and pray for liberation of the oppressed around the world. It is a day to cry out, "How long, O Lord, until all are free?" Many things in this world are a physical representation of a spiritual reality. The physical freedom and bondage we see today point us to the spiritual freedom and bondage that the gospel reveals as our ultimate reality. I will share the biblical basis for this kind of remembering on the Sabbath and then share some practical ways to model this for a Sunday worship service.

SABBATH IS A TIME TO REST

Deuteronomy 5:12 says, *"Observe the Sabbath day, to keep it holy, as the LORD your God commanded you."* The Exodus account of the Ten Commandments states God's example in creation as the reason for keeping the Sabbath. God rested, so we rest. But in Deuteronomy, God connects the Israelites' Sabbath with the deliverance from their bondage of slavery in Egypt as the reason to keep it. But the basic premise for the Sabbath is about rest.

> *"Six days you shall labor and do all your work, but the seventh day is a Sabbath to the LORD your God. On it you shall not do any work, you or your son or your daughter or your male servant or your female servant, or your ox or your donkey or any of your livestock, or the sojourner who is within your gates, that your male servant and your female servant may rest as well as you."* (Deuteronomy 5:13-14)

Sabbath is about resting from our regular work. In fact, the word *sabbath* means to "stop or cease" from doing something. The rhythm that God has given us is to work six days and rest one day. It is a day set aside to rest in God and delight in Him. This rest is a gift from God to His people, not a legalistic burden to bear, but a gift to be celebrated and enjoyed. Exodus 23:12 tells us that the Sabbath was given so that we may be refreshed. Redemptively, this rest points us ultimately to the eternal rest that is found only in Christ for all who trust in Him. True rest for our souls comes to those who rest in the work of Jesus on the cross. *"Come to me,"* Jesus says, *"all who labor and are heavy laden, and I will give you rest"* (Matthew 11:28).

SABBATH IS A TIME TO REMEMBER

On the Sabbath, we not only rest, but we also remember. What are we expected to remember? For one thing, we remember being slaves. *"You shall remember that **you were a slave in the land of Egypt**, and the LORD your God brought you out from there with a mighty hand and an outstretched arm"* (Deuteronomy 5:15, emphasis added). Part of keeping the Sabbath is remembering our former lives as slaves. Just as the Israelites were slaves in Egypt under Pharaoh, so we were once slaves to sin and Satan before meeting Christ. On this day we remember that once we were lost, but now we are found; we were blind, but now we see!

A second thing to remember on the Sabbath is that Jesus saves. Because of Christ, we are no longer a slave but a son and a daughter, and if the Son sets us free, we will be free indeed. It is a time to remember our history and our identity. Remember, we were slaves, but no more. Therefore we can rest. Why is resting so important on this day? It is significant to God, because failing to rest means we are still slaves to our work, which shows we are still living a life of slavery. For hundreds of years, the

Israelites were slaves in Egypt without the ability to rest, and God said, "No more! You are a son, not a slave. So rest and remember this truth of who you are." The Sabbath is a day to exalt Jesus Christ our Savior and Redeemer who has set us free from sin so we can rest in Him. That is why we gather. It is not about us, it is all about Jesus.

Thirdly, we remember on the Sabbath that we are not God. *"I am the Lord, and there is no other, besides me there is no God"* (Isaiah 45:5). When combined with faith, resting from work becomes an expression of trusting God. The Sabbath is an important time to rest and remember that God is God, and we are not. (And that's good news.) It is a reminder that all the things in our lives do not depend on us. If we are leaders, managers, or CEOs, this is an important reminder. I remembering hearing a parable that went like this:

A young boy was given a choice, to be either gigantic or tiny. He chose to be gigantic. His head brushed the clouds. He put his feet into the Atlantic Ocean as if it were a pond. He scooped whales with his fingers. With a few jumps, he went from one side of the country to the other. He kicked the top of a mountain like it was an anthill. He took a redwood tree and used it like a toothpick. When the boy got tired, he stretched out across Nebraska to Ohio, putting one arm in Colorado, and the other arm in Canada. It was magnificent and exhilarating . . . for about a day. Then it was boring. This gigantic boy then daydreamed about having made the other choice – to be minuscule instead. His backyard would have become an Amazonian rain forest. He could ride his hamster as if it were a woolly mammoth. He could fly as he rode on the back of a butterfly! A tub of ice cream would be a winter playground! Life would have been so much more interesting had he chosen smallness.

That is also a picture of what the Sabbath allows us to do. It is a time to rest in the greatness of who God is and that it is okay for us to be small. The only person who needs to be great is God. We do not need to be great, and we do not need to be the savior. We do not need to be in control of everything. That is God's job, and He is much better at it. The Sabbath is a day to be still and know that He is God.

A fourth thing to remember on the Sabbath is that there are many who cannot rest on this day. How is our Sabbath connected to justice? One way is to remember that there are millions today who cannot rest, though they desperately want to. We remember there are billions in the world who are still in spiritual slavery to sin. We remember that there are billions who have never heard of the name of Jesus. And we also need to remember there are more than thirty million people today who are physically enslaved because of the sins of others. On this day we remember that there are millions who cannot rest because of the slave driver who is using them and abusing them night and day. These victims cannot leave today, even if they wanted to, and that is slavery. It is a day to remember that the church has the only message that can truly set them free, not just physically, but also spiritually and for eternity. It is a declaration of the gospel message that will bring true freedom, for Jesus Christ is the Great Abolitionist.

SABBATH IS A TIME TO RESPOND

Isaiah teaches us about a further crucial aspect of honoring the Sabbath. In Isaiah 58, he highlights the powerful connection between the Sabbath and justice. In the subsequent chapter, we shall delve more deeply into Isaiah 58 in terms of fasting, but for now, I want to draw attention to the importance of justice in honoring the Sabbath. Let us look at this passage:

> *"If you turn back your foot from the Sabbath, from doing your pleasure on my holy day, and call the*

*Sabbath a delight and the holy day of the LORD hon-
orable; if you honor it, not going your own ways, or
seeking your own pleasure, or talking idly; then you
shall take delight in the LORD, and I will make you
ride on the heights of the earth; I will feed you with
the heritage of Jacob your father, for the mouth of
the LORD has spoken."* (Isaiah 58:13-14)

How are we to respond on the Sabbath? By learning to delight
in the Lord. As we rest in what the Lord has done and remember His goodness in our lives, the natural response will be to
worship and give thanks. Taking pleasure in the blessings that
God has given us in our life is one of the main aims of the gift
of the Sabbath – especially the gift of Himself. The opposite of
slavery in the Bible is not freedom, it is worshipping! Even in
the Exodus account, God tells Pharaoh to let the people go, so
that they may worship Him. We can rejoice in worship because
we have been set free from sin. We do not simply rejoice in our
own freedom, but we seek that freedom for others as well. Isaiah
58 shows us what fasting is supposed to look like. It is faith in
action; it is worship in action; it is love in action.

One group of churches in India operates the Asha Restoration
Home for girls who have come out of trafficking. Venkatamma is
one girl who was rescued. She lost her father when she was very
young. Her mother married at the age of fourteen and was forced
to work in the sex industry. The pimp overseeing her mom told
Venkatamma that he could provide a good-paying job for her in
another city. But as she was being transferred on a train to that new
job in a new city, she overheard the men saying they planned to sell
her to other traffickers in another city. She escaped from the train,
and by God's grace, she was led to Asha Restoration Home. It was
through this ministry that she was helped, restored, and trained
as both a tailor and a beautician. Through this ministry, she was

given a new hope and a new future. It was also in this ministry that she was told of the love that Jesus Christ had for her. After eight months in this rescue home, she gave her life to Jesus and was baptized. Why did this happen? Because the church in India remembered that there are vulnerable youth in their community who need the love of Jesus, and they knew they were the ones to share that love with their community. They responded from the place of worshipping Jesus to showing others the love of Jesus.

CELEBRATING FREEDOM SUNDAY

How do we implement a Freedom Sunday in our church? First, once a year, dedicate a weekend at your church to focus on God's heart for justice.

SONGS
Begin with songs that lift up and exalt the greatness of who our God is. Then sing songs that reflect the heart of God for our world. You can also incorporate songs that cry out for His deliverance and saving grace.

PRAYERS
During the prayer portions of your service, lift up those who are enslaved and pray for their freedom and healing. Pray also for the pimps, traffickers, and johns who are in bondage to the sin that is driving this industry. Then pray for the church to rise up and be the light and love of Jesus to bring change in our communities. Finally, pray for an end to human trafficking and modern-day slavery in our lifetime.

SERMON
The pastor can preach on God's heart for justice, His heart for the oppressed and vulnerable, or the slavery that exists

today – both physically and spiritually. This is a biblical issue and a reflection of demonstrating the gospel of Jesus Christ to our world. This can also be a Sunday where you invite a guest speaker from an organization that has been working in this arena to share from Scripture and testimonies from the field. We often update our congregation on the lives that have been changed the past year through the church's efforts.

OFFERING
You can take up a special love offering this weekend and donate it to an aftercare center, organization, or project that is dedicated to helping trafficked victims.

RESPONSE
After reading through this book and especially the chapters on what the church can do, select one or two practical next steps your church can take in being a part of the solution to this problem. Introduce these steps at the end of the service to give your congregation an opportunity to walk in faith and obedience after hearing the message.

THAT THEY MAY SEE YOUR GOOD DEEDS

Back in 2011, when we did our first Freedom Sunday, there were no other churches (that I knew of) that had a weekend focused on this issue. We announced this special Sunday several weeks prior, so that friends and neighbors could join us. There was a surprise inquiry about our Freedom Sunday a few weeks beforehand from CNN International, who wanted to cover that service. We were surprised and delighted to have someone from the mainstream media not only cover but also broadcast parts of our service that day. CNN is traditionally a breaking-news network, which means they only report on events that are taking place right now. But in 2011, the news network made the decision to use their platform and resources to address a problem, and the problem they chose was human trafficking. As a result, they were intrigued by a church also tackling the same problem.

In the months to follow, after we started our justice ministry, we were contacted by government officials from Korea, the United States, and other countries. Representatives from the U.S. Senate and Congress toured East Asia to see what was being done to help vulnerable groups, and they asked us for a meeting. It became clear that, though these groups did not normally set up meetings with churches, they were drawn to our ministry because we were actively involved in these areas of injustice. We were seeing a glimpse of what Jesus meant when he said, *"Let your light shine before others, so that they may see your good works and give glory to your Father who is in heaven"* (Matthew 5:16).

I read a biography of Steve Jobs not too long ago. It was an interesting read and a wonderful story of the blessing of adoption. His biological parents contemplated abortion, but decided instead to give him up for adoption. One of the things that stood out to me was the reason Steve Jobs left the church.

He attended a Lutheran church as a boy. One day he saw an issue of *Life* magazine that featured a shocking cover story of the starving children in Nigeria. He took the magazine to his Sunday school teacher and asked if God knew this was happening. His teacher replied to Steve that God knows everything. But Steve could not understand why no one was helping these children. If God knew this urgent problem, then why wasn't His church involved in feeding the hungry in Nigeria? If God is love, then why wasn't His church expressing that love to the hurting world? The Sunday school teacher was left without any answers to Steve's impassioned questions. The silence from the teacher and the church's absence in a needy world is what led Steve Jobs to leave the church. He said that Christianity loses its power when we talk too much without living like Jesus or seeing the world as Jesus saw it.

His heart was longing to see Jesus through His body, the church. He was crying out to see the church in action around the world. That is the cry of many around the world today. They are crying out, "God, if you are real, show yourself to me!" We, the church – the body of Christ – are to be the answer to that prayer. The world is longing to see Jesus – in us. May the church rise up in this hour and see a glimpse of Jesus in us.

GROUP DISCUSSION QUESTIONS:

- Share something that stood out to you in this chapter in terms of what we are called upon to remember on the Sabbath.

- Is remembering that we were once slaves still relevant to us today? Or is it only for the Israelites in Exodus? Why do you think so?

- Has your church ever held a Freedom Sunday? If so, share what you found to be significant about it. If not, what are ways you could incorporate some of these elements into a future service?

PRAYER GUIDE:

- Thank God for the freedom we have been given through the sacrifice of Jesus.

- Pray for more churches to participate in Freedom Sunday and reveal God's heart for justice in our world.

- Pray for your church to be a change agent in your city – a city on a hill that cannot be hidden.

CHAPTER 8

WHAT THE CHURCH CAN DO

"In the same way, let your light shine before others, so that they may see your good works and give glory to your Father who is in heaven." (Matthew 5:16)

Lack of citizenship is the chief factor in the particular vulnerability of hill-tribe women and girls to trafficking and other forms of exploitation.[53]

All that is necessary for the triumph of evil is for good men to do nothing. (This is often attributed to Edmund Burke.)

A JUSTICE MINISTRY IS BORN: HOPE BE RESTORED

When I first became aware of the problem of human trafficking, practical ways of how our church could get involved popped into my mind during my brainstorming sessions with God. My anger against the injustice turned into excitement because of the possibilities of what could be and

---

53   "Hill Tribe Citizenship," *https://tinyurl.com/2zce9zzu* (March 11, 2023).

what should be in our world. I bathed these ideas in prayer for a few weeks, and soon thereafter the idea behind HOPE Be Restored was born. In the days ahead, this freedom-and-justice ministry in our church pioneered a new movement for Korea. Before I share what HOPE Be Restored does, I want to share about the significance of the name.

HOPE Be Restored stands for "Helping the Oppressed and Prisoners of injustice Escape and Be Restored." Our aim is to help, heal, and restore lives through the power of God's love and the gospel of Jesus Christ. But more important than that, it is a declaration. It declares to this world that hope will be restored. It is a verbal declaration of faith of what we believe will be the end result in our world. We believe that the lives of those who are living in hopelessness will find hope again. We declare by faith that hope will rise up out of the darkest night.

SIX KEY AREAS TO FOCUS ON AS A JUSTICE MINISTRY:

1. PRAYER TEAM

Ending human trafficking begins with prayer. The more I've been involved in this issue, the more I realize that the first line of battle must be fought on our knees. This involves intense spiritual warfare, and it must be fought in the spiritual realm. Prayer has great power because it takes us into the presence of God to commune with Him. Prayer is the means through which God chooses to release His power into the world. Therefore, we believe prayer is a vital part of ending modern-day slavery.

As a result, the first team we formed in our justice ministry was our prayer team. This team is dedicated to praying for the injustices to end and for people to be set free, but their role is also to find ways to increase prayers from the church and to help people pray more effectively. The HBR prayer team created prayer guides to aid the church in prayer. We felt convicted that we must not only pray in our homes and in our churches but also in the streets of our city. On a weekly or monthly basis, our prayer teams participated in prayer walks through the streets of the city that have known sex-trafficking activity. We hold prayer and fasting chains for extended periods of time, sometimes up to forty days, because we understand the intense spiritual nature of the war that we are fighting.

In all this, we seek to tear down the spiritual strongholds that are connected to human trafficking, such as greed, lust, and pride. Prayer is the cornerstone of this ministry because prayer keeps us connected to Christ, and Christ is the cornerstone for the church.

2. AWARENESS TEAM

After we established our prayer team, the next logical step was to create an awareness team. Human trafficking has gained much attention in recent years, but many are still unaware or have misconceptions about modern-day slavery. So the awareness team is dedicated to raising awareness within our community – elementary schools, middle schools, high schools, colleges, churches, military bases, and any other place where people are willing to listen. Our church in Korea hosted an annual justice conference to raise awareness and equip churches to join this fight to eliminate human trafficking. We also partner with several aftercare centers to hold campaigns in the streets of Seoul to let the public know what is happening to the millions of trafficked victims in our city. Though the journey towards justice begins with awareness, it must not end there.

David Batstone, the co-founder and president of Not for Sale, first encountered slavery in his own backyard when he discovered in the newspaper that his favorite Indian restaurant in San Francisco shut down after the police discovered the restaurant used trafficked children to serve the tables and work in the kitchen. This shocking discovery led him on a journey around the world to find out how widespread slavery was. After months of research and interviews, he realized that he could no longer live life as usual while millions were enslaved in our day and age. As a result, *Not for Sale* was written and a new organization to end slavery was born. Awareness can be a powerful tool to open eyes and change the course of a life.

3. RESEARCH TEAM

In order to raise awareness effectively, we need good data to support our message. We have a team to gather this data and research trafficking cases that happen within our city. This team monitors trends and maps out key areas in our community where trafficking happens. With this data, we are able to know where to pray and how to pray more effectively, thereby aiding our prayer team. The research team collects stories of victims and statistics from newspapers and police reports and compiles them into reports for the public to use. As a result, they are able to help our awareness team with the most recent and relevant information to share during our awareness campaigns. The research team also inputs trafficking cases into a database that documents convictions that happen around the world.

4. NETWORKING TEAM

Another key component of our ministry is to network and build relationships with strategic partners who can help us bring an end to these injustices. We network with churches, government officials, law enforcement, lawyers, CEOs, celebrities, and other organizations who share this passion to bring change in our cities. Human trafficking is a huge global problem today, and it's going to take a global network of people working together to bring this evil to an end. These traffickers know how to network with other industries, such as travel agents, border patrol, taxi drivers, and even grocery-store owners. If they know how to network and work well with others, how much more should we! We need to partner with each other and pool our relationship resources together. We are in this together and we need each other if we're going to see this evil end within our lifetime.

5. RESTORATION TEAM

A central part of our mission is to help restore hope and bring healing through the gospel of Jesus Christ. We believe the gospel must be declared and demonstrated. They must hear about God's love, but they also need to experience God's love through His body – the church.

Through prayer, counseling, and friendships, we support safe houses and aftercare centers where lives are able to be healed physically, emotionally, and spiritually. These places provide new job skills and educational opportunities so they have tools to help them build a bright new chapter in their lives.

We also started the House of Hope restoration center, which was one of the first Christ-centered aftercare homes in Korea. It provides free housing, counseling, and care for single moms (who are one of the most vulnerable groups to traffickers) and survivors of trafficking.

6. OUTREACH TEAM

We not only want to help survivors, but we also want to prevent this from occurring. In our rescue efforts, we partner with experienced aftercare workers in our city to build relationships with sex-trafficking victims to let them know that there are people ready to help them at a moment's notice. We go to areas of high vulnerability, both in Korea and other countries, in order to educate the young children and women and to protect them before they fall into the hands of traffickers.

WHAT CAN WE DO?

The most common question I receive from pastors and church leaders is, What can we do as a church?

There's a lot you can do! In fact, you have one of the most important roles to play in the abolition of modern-day slavery. As we've clearly seen, at its core, slavery is a spiritual issue that must be dealt with in the spiritual realm. If you are a spiritual leader, this is your battleground. If God leads, I would encourage you to begin a justice ministry in your church that has one or multiple components of ideas found within this chapter. The church can lead in multiple ways.

TEACH AND PREACH

SERMONS

The power of pulpit ministry must be utilized to raise up a new generation of abolitionists who are grounded in Scripture, persistent in prayer, and willing to follow in the footsteps of Jesus. I would encourage pastors and leaders to speak on the issues connected to human trafficking in their preaching and teaching. Provide the biblical groundwork for the congregation to know that this is a biblical issue and a timely one for the church to be engaged in. The issues we are up against concerning human trafficking are core spiritual issues, such as the greed that lures traffickers into this arena, the lust of the johns, and the self-hatred that overcomes many victims.

To help get your congregation on board, I suggest doing a sermon series on biblical justice and introduce the issues of human trafficking. This type of series could encompass topics such as love for our neighbors, lust that enslaves, and mercy towards the weak. It could include missions in the darkest places of the world, compassion for the suffering, freedom for spiritual captives, and justice as an expression of love. Slavery that is not only physical bondage but also spiritual and emotional bondage, greed as the source of all kinds of evil, and ultimately, how true love and freedom can be found in the mission, message, and person of Jesus Christ are also topics to be covered in a sermon series.

If preaching a series seems too daunting of a task to begin with, you could start with a justice-themed weekend like Freedom Sunday, which designates one Sunday out of the year to remember the millions around the world who are enslaved to this physical and spiritual bondage. Be it through a sermon or a series, the pastor has an important role to play in casting a vision of what biblical justice looks like through the local church.

STUDY - PERSONAL AND GROUP

SMALL GROUP BIBLE STUDIES
Doing a small group Bible study on the various issues connected to justice (freedom, sin, mercy, bondage) can help get your church to study the issues biblically and discuss ways to take action within the community. Even doing a word study on *justice* throughout Scripture will reveal much of God's heart for the weak and the oppressed and make it clear that the church is to be a reflection of that heart to our world.

STUDYING HISTORY
From looking at the Exodus account in Scripture to exploring the work of William Wilberforce in abolishing the British slave trade, studying the history of past abolitionist movements is another way to raise awareness and gain inspiration from church leaders who have gone before us. It's fascinating to note that previous justice movements were spearheaded by the church. (See Appendix 1 for a list of resources on books.)

SCREENING FILMS

Some excellent documentaries give an overview of human trafficking and include inspirational testimonies of what God is doing to set people free. *Nefarious: Merchant of Souls* by Exodus Cry, and *At the End of Slavery: The Battle for Justice in Our Time* by the International Justice Mission provide a solid introduction to trafficking. *Save My Seoul* is a documentary on sex trafficking in South Korea to help people understand the complexities of this issue in Korea, as well as dispel common lies people believe about how women end up in the industry. Having movie nights or incorporating these films into a conference setting can be a powerful tool in raising awareness.

PRAYER

Justice flows from God's throne into our world in many ways. It can come through the judicial systems of the world. It can come through law enforcement. But another way we are to seek justice is through persistent, faith-filled prayers to the God of justice. Bethany Hoang of International Justice Mission reminds us that "At the end of the day, if our attempts to seek justice do not first begin with the work of prayer, we will be worn and weary."[54]

> And he told them a parable to the effect that they ought always to pray and not lose heart. He said, "In a certain city there was a judge who neither feared God nor respected man. And there was a widow in that city who kept coming to him and saying, 'Give me justice against my adversary.' For a while he refused, but afterward he said to himself, 'Though I neither fear God nor respect man, yet because this

---

54   Hoang, *Deepening the Soul for Justice*, 7.

widow keeps bothering me, I will give her justice,
so that she will not beat me down by her continual
coming.' And the Lord said, "Hear what the unrigh-
teous judge says. And will not God give justice to his
elect, who cry to him day and night? Will he delay
long over them? I tell you, he will give justice to
them speedily. Nevertheless, when the Son of Man
comes, will he find faith on earth?" (Luke 18:1-8)

The ultimate answer to our prayers for justice is the return of Jesus, the righteous Judge who will make right all wrongs.

PRIORITY OF PRAYER

Prayer is a powerful weapon in the fight for freedom. Jesus tells us that it is through persistent, faith-filled prayer that God will bring forth justice to His elect (Luke 18:7). Much of the heavy fighting takes place in the unseen arena of spiritual warfare. Prayer changes things, and it is prayer that can bring transformation in the spiritual dimensions of a community.

International Justice Mission understands the utter importance of prayer in this battle, so they begin their workdays with thirty minutes of silence and prayer and then gather again at 11:00 a.m. to pray together as a group as they seek the Lord's help.[55] As a result, they have seen many breakthroughs in trafficking cases around the world and have found favor from influential supporters. May everyone in the church pray on a regular basis for the end of human trafficking in our lifetime.

PRAYER TOPICS

Provide your church with some practical steps on how to pray for this issue. The list of items to pray for can become quite extensive, but here are several topics to begin with:

---

55   Gary Haugen, *Just Courage: God's Great Expedition for the Restless Christian* (Downers Grove: IVP Books, 2008), 23.

- *Pray for the victims.* Pray for all who are bound physically and spiritually to be set free and pray that they will be healed and restored in Jesus' name.

- *Pray for the traffickers.* Pray that they would repent of their sins and turn from their wicked ways. Pray that they too would be set free from their bondage to greed and find the greatest treasure to pursue – Jesus Christ.

- *Pray for justice in the justice system.* With corruption being a factor that allows trafficking to take place in many parts of the world, pray that those who are in positions of power and influence would do the right thing in upholding the law and protecting the vulnerable. Pray that justice would reign in the law enforcement and judicial systems of the world.

- *Pray for the "breaking grounds" to be destroyed.* The breaking grounds are one of the darkest and most hideous places on the planet – where victims of sex trafficking are "seasoned" for the profession of prostitution through violent means of sexual assault, physical abuse, and drugs. Pray in Jesus' name that the police will find these places and every breaking ground will disappear from this planet.

- *Pray for organizations on the frontlines.* Pray for protection, provision, and success as groups around the world fight on behalf of the oppressed. Pray for effectiveness as they seek to educate, rescue, and restore the vulnerable in these nations. Pray that they will be strengthened with joy for their difficult journey of seeing justice established in places where corruption often runs rampant.

- *Pray for the church to rise up.* Pray that the church will awaken from its slumber towards justice issues and be the leading force in declaring and demonstrating the gospel to a world in darkness.

- *Pray for more intercessors.* Pray that God will raise up more people to pray and intercede for justice to be established in every nation. Pray that God will raise up prayer houses in your city. Pray that God will raise up intercessors who will contend night and day until the captives are set free.

- *Repent for the sins we have committed.* Pray for repentance for the ways that we have sinned by our lust, our greed, and our selfishness. Confess the sins of the church and of our nation. Before we condemn the sinner "over there," let us confess the sins in our own hearts.

- *Pray for the end of human trafficking and modern-day slavery.* Let us be specific and intentional about praying for the end of this great evil and injustice in our lifetime. May we extinguish this evil and not leave it as an inheritance to the next generation.

PRAYER IDEAS

It is important to get your church to pray for this issue. A key question to ask is, How can we increase prayer? Here are some suggestions:

Partner with your prayer ministry. One of the most important ministries in this movement for freedom and justice is your church's prayer ministry. There is power in prayer, and as more prayers go up, more strongholds will come down. While we want everyone to pray for freedom and justice, it is wise to begin with those gifted with intercession and those who have a heart for prayer.

Prayer walk in your community. Our church has a monthly prayer walk where we go to key areas of influence in our city (city hall, supreme court, etc.) and pray against any injustices and for blessings on our community. We also send out more seasoned and experienced intercessory teams to pray in areas of darkness or areas known for sex trafficking; but extreme wisdom, caution, and supervision is strongly recommended before sending any team out to a potentially dangerous area. This is intense spiritual warfare, so be prayerful and careful as you follow God's lead in this area.

Several years ago, some of our team members did a prayer walk through Gangnam every second and fourth Tuesday. The area is a lively spot for nightlife with hidden, unassuming venues for prostitution nearby. The sidewalks are littered with small business cards and flyers for massage parlors, adult internet cyber rooms, and room salons. One of the prayer walkers reported this:

"Not long into it, we noticed a profound decline in prostitution ads on the ground in the area. And it came to our attention that there had been a huge bust on those printing those ads. Also, a few months into praying for the area, it was seen in the news that the city had ordered a mass investigation into the loan sharks of Gangnam, something that we had been praying for extensively.

"We also saw some businesses that operated prostitution rings shut down after months of praying for their end. Some may see it as a coincidence, but we learned that the more we pray, and the more specifically we pray, the more 'coincidences' we will see in our lives."

Join a 24/7 prayer chain. Your church can create its own prayer chain or join prayer groups that are already engaged in this.

FASTING

A BIBLICAL FAST
Isaiah 58 tells us that our fasting should not be just giving up our food, but also feeding others who are without food. It is a time to seek out justice within our communities. Verse 6 of the chapter says, *"Is not this the fast that I choose: to loosen the bonds of wickedness, to undo the straps of the yoke, to let the oppressed go free, and to break every yoke?"*

A God-honoring fast is not just giving up something we need; it also seeks to meet the needs of others, especially those who are oppressed. It is choosing to suffer in this small way so we might gain a heart of compassion for the sufferings of others. You might consider participating in one of these fasts:

Personal Fast. I know many people who have been led by God to do an extended period of personal fasting for the sins of the nation and the freedom of the captives. Whether it is one meal, one day, or longer, pray that our longing for food would be replaced by a greater longing for Jesus, His return, and justice in our world.

Corporate Fast. During the season of Lent, our church went through a Fast for Freedom. This was a forty-day fast of giving up one meal per day, Monday to Saturday, from Ash Wednesday to Easter Sunday. During this fast, instead of eating a meal, we spent that time praying for revival, freedom, and justice.

In addition to giving up one meal per day, we set aside the money we would have used on that meal and donated it to a freedom project. Our first Fast for Freedom raised about $75,000, and we were able to give that money to help buy land and build a new dorm for children in Northern Thailand who are survivors of human trafficking. During another campaign, the money raised went towards college scholarships for stateless children in Northern Thailand. In Thailand, if a stateless child can graduate from college, they are given citizenship and a whole new world of opportunity.

Slavery Fast. Another idea is to have the church fast from slavery-made foods and products. Many of the major chocolate companies use slave labor to pick the cocoa beans that make up chocolate. Giving up those brands in favor of companies that use slave-free chocolate can be a practical way to impact the industry. You can visit www.slavefreechocolate.org for a list of companies that use ethically grown cocoa.

OTHER CHURCH MINISTRIES TO GET INVOLVED IN

MEN'S MINISTRY

At one of our first justice conferences, a man in the audience raised his hand. "What can men do to help stem this tide of sex trafficking?" he asked.

The speaker, a woman with decades of experience in the field, didn't bat an eye. "Stop watching pornography," she said.

The consumption of porn and prostitution is fueled by lust, and for men, that starts in the privacy of not only their home computer but also within their hearts. Also, the porn industry is closely tied to sex trafficking. Exodus Cry, www.exoduscry.com, has created a number of resources (articles and films) that show the connection between those two industries.

Involvement in justice work not only spurs men to greater personal holiness because they witness the direct impact that lust has on women, but it also provides a positive focal point for realizing that to break the chains of human trafficking in this world, men need to learn how to be men of God.

If we want to root out the demand, we need to help men become the men that God intended them to be. Instead of being enslaved to porn and sexual perversion, the heart needs an encounter with the gospel of Jesus Christ so that it will be free to honor sex as a gift to be enjoyed in the context of the marriage covenant between husband and wife.

Suggestions for a men's ministry:

Provide accountability. In a world where sexually provocative images are on display wherever we look, men need a place to share their struggles and find support now more than ever. Having one-on-one mentoring or small groups of accountability will be a gift to offer the men of your church. Let the men of your church form their own anti-porn community and fight for purity and honor together.

Mobilize and mentor men of valor. Creating a new culture where purity and fidelity is honored is bringing the kingdom of God to your church. Men of valor who will be courageous and strong, seeking to be defenders of the weak and the oppressed, are needed at this hour. For too long, we have allowed Hollywood or *Playboy* to define what a man looks like. We need a new generation of men committed to Christ and His Word to show the next generation that Jesus is the ultimate definition of manhood. Have godly men mentor the younger men of your church and teach them that they were created to be a source of protection for women, not a supporter of exploitation. We are living in a critical hour where men of godly courage are hard to find. It is time to disciple boys to be true men in Christ.

Share the gospel with the men of your city. Hearts can only change through the power of the gospel, and we need to offer the good news to every man, woman, and child in our cities. Since men are driving the demand for sex trafficking around the world, when the hearts of men change, this situation will change. Share the gospel today, and let us pray for a revival of the men in our generation.

WOMEN'S MINISTRY

Encourage women to consider volunteering at local aftercare centers, since the victims are often women. Women can be involved in this issue through prayer, fundraising, and even mentoring the younger girls in your community.

ORPHAN-CARE MINISTRY

Orphans are some of the most vulnerable people in the world to fall into the hands of traffickers. With no one looking out for them, especially after they leave the institutional system, they are left to fend for themselves. Sadly, in some countries traffickers wait until girls "age out" of the orphanages, and then they recruit them for their own businesses. Establishing a church ministry that will care for the orphans through foster care, adoption, and mentoring programs is another way to not only love the vulnerable with the love of Jesus but also protect a group of people who are often a target for traffickers. Caring for orphans is one of the best preventative measures in this fight against trafficking.

Recently, a local orphanage ran out of funds and had to close down. One of the workers at the orphanage who knew that our church had a heart for orphans contacted me and asked if anyone in our church could become foster parents for one of their twelve-year-old girls who had nowhere to go. I already knew too well that sending a twelve-year-old girl with no family support onto the streets was a trafficking story waiting to happen, so without even asking our church members, I told the orphanage worker that I guaranteed someone in our church would care for her. I called one couple in our community, Kent and Daisy, and explained the situation, and I asked if they'd be open to being foster parents for this young girl. They prayed about it for a day, and the next afternoon they called me and said that they would care for her. I was overjoyed at their quick response to care for an orphan in need and especially a young child who would be left extremely vulnerable if no one came through. Orphan care in the church is a vital part of loving our neighbors, valuing the vulnerable, and preventing tragic stories from happening.

YOUTH GROUP

Take advantage of the passion that teens have and release them to use that energy to raise awareness of this issue within your church and community. This generation of youth is wired to live their lives with purpose and to respond passionately in living their lives to help others.

CHILDREN'S MINISTRY

I used to think that our children were too young to understand the issues of justice and freedom, but I was wrong. Even very young children have a strong sense of justice. Simply give a child less candy than the child next to her, and she will inevitably cry out, "That's not fair!" Children know what is right, wrong, and fair. Teaching them about sex trafficking is probably not a good idea at this age, but telling them about child slave labor is something that they can connect with.

I had the opportunity to share how children in Africa are sometimes victims of child slave labor. They are forced to pick cocoa beans, which in turn are used to make many of our chocolates. The result of the simple talk? One of the fifth-grade girls named Esther compiled a list of all the grades that the chocolate companies received, and she distributed it to all of her classmates at school. As a result, Esther and her friends have decided not to buy slavery-made chocolate anymore. I do not know if I could have done that as a young fifth grader myself, but I was proud to see how, at such a young age, she not only understood the issue, but she also took a stand and became a voice for these African children. Now we have a bunch of fifth-grade abolitionists who are already influencing their generation to make changes! You can see a copy of her chocolate report card at the HOPE Be Restored website (www.hopeberestored.org).

Another time, I spoke at the chapel at Los Gatos Christian School in Los Gatos, California, which is a K-8 school. It was right before Halloween, and I shared about God's heart for justice. I told them that many companies use child slave labor to pick those cocoa beans that make up our chocolate. The fourth-grade class was so convicted by this that they gave up their slave-labor Halloween chocolate and brought it to school – almost ten pounds' worth! One of the teachers dropped it off at my office, and we were all just blown away. Children understand justice. They get it because they are made in the image of God, who is a God of justice.

SINGLE-MOMS' MINISTRY
It may not be the case for all countries, but in South Korea where I pastored for twelve years, the young single-mom population is growing, and they are extremely vulnerable. Currently in South Korea there are over two hundred thousand young single moms with children under the age of eighteen. Most say financial difficulty is their biggest challenge, with the average monthly income ranging between $500 and $1,000. A survey showed that most of these moms have to borrow money each month to make ends meet, and 22 percent borrow $300 to $1,000 per month for living costs. Because of the increasing debts they face each month, a large number give up their children for adoption even though they do not want to. They simply can't

afford to keep their children. And even if they give up their children, they are still faced with a large debt that they must somehow pay off.

For many of these moms, because of the debt they incur and the limited education they have (most do not have a high school education), they are unable to get a proper loan from banks. In times of desperation, they often turn to loan sharks who charge large sums of interest – sometimes more than 300 percent interest on their loans! Getting deeper and deeper into debt, some of these women are forced into the sex industry as a means of paying back their creditors.

One of the most heartbreaking things our teams have reported during their prayer walks and visits to the red-light districts is seeing the scattered toys and children's clothes hanging outside the brothels. One of our members said this:

"There were also the toy stores and children's clothes in Yongjugol (a red-light district) that are on display and sometimes seen in the brothels themselves. In that, I saw how these women are still trying to have a normal life, how they're still trying to love their children."

So as another preventative measure to care for this vulnerable group (both for the mom and the orphans), our church began a ministry called Single Love that provides free diapers, baby clothes, food, childcare, tutoring help, mentoring, and friendships so these young moms can be encouraged to keep going and dream great dreams for themselves and their children.

I encourage you to look into your community and find out who the vulnerable people are. It may be the teen runaways; it may be the orphans; it may be the single moms. Simply love them, serve them, and meet their needs. In doing so, they might see a clearer picture of Jesus too.

MISSION PROJECTS

SHORT-TERM MISSIONS

Along with traditional short-term missions trips, our church also provides opportunities to go on missions trips that serve organizations that are on the frontlines in this fight for freedom. From providing English lessons to doing Vacation Bible School to simply cleaning the facilities, serving those who are rescuing and restoring survivors of trafficking is always an honor. Youth with a Mission (YWAM) also provides a Discipleship Training School (DTS) program that has a justice track for its outreach. Those who would like to commit to several months of service can consider this option.

LONG-TERM MISSIONS

For churches who are actively engaged in sending out long-term missionaries and establishing cross-cultural church plants overseas, I would suggest they prayerfully consider planting churches in regions of the world where trafficking frequently happens. The light of the body of Christ needs to be established in these dark places.

Our church is praying about church planting in Isaan, the northeastern part of Thailand. Some surveys have said that up to 80 percent of the women working in the red-light districts of Thailand are from this region. Also, some parts of Eastern Europe, such as Moldova, are seeing a major increase in orphans due to economic instability, leading to many young children and girls being trafficked. It would be wonderful to see churches begin showing up in these places to lead the way in providing safety and solutions.

Above all else, wherever you see great darkness in the hearts of men, the light of the gospel needs to be all the more present in these places. We need to continually plant churches and worship in dark places.

CASE STUDY: AGAPE INTERNATIONAL
MISSIONS (CAMBODIA)

Agape International Missions is a pioneer church in the fight against sex trafficking that is bringing transformation in Cambodia. Don Brewster, the founder and director of AIM, realized that the only way to drive out darkness is to bring the light and love of Jesus into these dark communities. This church decided it needed to live in areas where trafficking was taking place and to become a part of the community. As a result, they were able to befriend the locals and gather crucial information that led to the rescue and restoration of hundreds of girls in their area. They do three key things: fight trafficking, restore victims, and transform communities.

First of all, they fight human trafficking. One key way they do this is through The Lord's Gym, which is a free workout center where their staff builds relationships with traffickers. As relationships are formed, opportunities to share the good news of the gospel arise, and the evil of trafficking is brought to their attention. Invitations are given to traffickers to attend church and to receive prayer. Here is a powerful testimony of what happened to one trafficker after his time in The Lord's Gym:

Sokunthy was notorious for trafficking young girls. Every day, he attended The Lord's Gym where he was prayed for by the staff. He heard the truth about the evil he was perpetuating within the community and was invited to church. One day, AIM was called to help two very young girls who had been raped by their brother. Their brother was Sokunthy. When he didn't come to the gym the following day, AIM's pastor went and told him, "You know we hate what you did. But the truth is, the gym is the Lord's gym. And no matter what you've done, He'll forgive you. We want you to come back."

He came back the next day and agreed to go to church. Once there, he stood up and said, "I know what I was doing was wrong, and I am never going to do it again." AIM discipled him and helped him get a new job where he makes a clean fifty dollars a month compared to the thousands he would make in trafficking. Through the power of prayer and the working of God's Holy Spirit, he has not hurt another child and is completely transformed.[56]

Another way they fight trafficking is through an anti-trafficking training program that they offer to the church body. This eight-session workshop describes ways to create a prevention plan, ways to cut off the supply, ways to confront the demand, and aftercare strategies. You can request training even in your own church by visiting their website.

The second key part of their ministry is restoring the victims of sex trafficking through their Agape Restoration Center (ARC) and the Agape Training Center (ATC). The ARC is where they seek to meet the physical, psychosocial, educational, vocational, and spiritual needs of those rescued. They are given a safe place to live, nutritious meals, counseling, therapy, education, job skills, and spiritual feeding for their holistic growth. The ATC provides new career opportunities for these young women to gain new income and experience a new level of self-worth and dignity. Here is a testimony from someone who came out of ARC:

Mi arrived at ARC at the age of twelve after being sold by her mother and abused physically, sexually, and emotionally for years. Through the loving guidance of Mi's counselors and house moms, hope blossomed in Mi's heart, and she accepted Jesus as her Lord. She applied herself in her academic studies and vocational training, landing a job in a high-profile bakery. Now she creates beautiful cakes for the prime minister and the king and earns enough to support herself and her siblings. "I was so happy when I lived at ARC," Mi writes. "Although being

---

56 Handley, Erin, and Muong, Vandy, and Sunjolinet, Bora, "The Lord's Gym: Where even sex traffickers are welcome to work out," *The Phnom Penh Post: https://tinyurl.com/5x6vaana* (July 29, 2016).

at home has many struggles, yet they motivate me to be firm and strong and persevere in dealing with my life circumstances. Every day when I come back from work, I teach the poor kids in my community how to read and write so they can live good. I sacrificially lay out my lifestyle to help those kids like ARC helps me, no matter how trivial my problem. Now I can help others, and I do it with everything I have and all of my heart."[57]

A third part of AIM's strategy to fight trafficking is through the transformation of communities. They offer a Kids' Club that teaches literacy, English, life skills, Bible stories, arts, crafts, and music to more than four hundred children in their community. There is Rahab's House Church that is a Christ-centered, Bible-teaching community church providing worship and discipleship. They provide quality healthcare through a clinic that is made available to all people in their community. And they have a community school that teaches reading, math, life skills, and ESL (English as a Second Language).

The successful fruit of these ministries has resulted in church plants and church networks with over a thousand village churches throughout Cambodia. These are all ways that the gospel is both demonstrated and declared in Cambodia. The people have experienced the verbal and visible witness of the church, and lives are being saved, and communities are being transformed.

The exciting part about AIM's story is that every church can do similar ministries within their own community. We don't have to get on an airplane to do the mission that God has given His people to do. We begin by being light wherever God has placed us to be. Research your community and find out who the vulnerable are and begin serving them. *The Just Church* by Jim Martin gives some practical advice on forming

---

57   Testimony of AIM survivors: *https://aimfree.org/hope-stories-mi/.*

an action plan against the injustices of your community and how to engage your area for justice as a church.

CONNECT AND COLLABORATE

FRIENDSHIPS
With wisdom and guidance from your leadership at church, prayerfully seek the Lord's guidance for some of the women in your church to befriend the women who are working in the red-light districts or other areas of prostitution in your communities. Please use caution depending on the safety risks involved. Only spiritually mature and sensitive people should attempt this type of ministry. It is not for everyone, but I believe the Lord will guide some women and churches to love and befriend these women just like Jesus did.

NETWORK TOGETHER
Bring together the various professions within your congregation and brainstorm to see what you can do as a networking freedom community. Few places in the world have such a diverse group of professions gathered together on a weekly basis as a church. Great potential for synergy and creative ideas exists in such a gathering. The possibilities of these collaborations are numerous:

Resource provision. Take some of the entrepreneurial business members of your congregation on a vision trip to some of these poorer areas of the world where trafficking happens. Challenge them to come up with ideas for new business ventures to create new job opportunities for many of those who are vulnerable to traffickers. Great ideas often come from pooling resources and brainstorming with God and His people.

Some people have donated their extra summer home to an aftercare center so women who were victims of trafficking could have a safe place to stay during their restoration period. Others who own their own businesses or are CEOs of companies have offered entry-level jobs and job training for these survivors to begin a new life.

Network with other churches. Learn from other churches that are taking steps in their community to fight this problem. Join together with churches to have a joint worship or prayer meeting to declare freedom in your city. That unity would not only be a powerful witness to the world, but it would also bring great delight to the Father's heart.

Vocational collaboration. In the church that I am pastoring, our Korean-speaking congregation formed a group called the Christian CEO Forum. This group of high-level business leaders gathers on a weekly basis for fellowship breakfasts, midweek discipleship, and quarterly conferences in order to brainstorm solutions for the greatest levels of changes they can bring for the greatest good. When gifted leaders are given a problem, their natural bent towards problem-solving can create some innovative solutions. Take advantage of how the leaders of your congregation are wired and bring them together to solve some of the greatest problems of our generation.

In addition to business leaders, other professionals can work together to use their area of expertise to tackle this issue. For example, we have many teachers in our congregation, and they formed a Teachers Abolitionist Movement. One of the tools they've created is a curriculum series to teach grade schools, middle schools, and high schools on human trafficking and modern-day slavery. Students have also started clubs in their schools that raise awareness and do fundraising drives. We have lawyers who volunteer their services to help victims process their legal forms and inform them of their rights. Every profession can do something to change society for the better.

This is what Jesus means by being salt and light. It's about being a change agent in the place where God puts you.

One factor that strengthened William Wilberforce to persevere in his fight for justice while serving in the British parliament was his involvement with the Clapham Sect. This was a group of influential Christian business leaders and government workers who came together to use their platforms and networks to bring about social change. They realized God had put them all into positions of power in order to use their platforms to influence change within their society.

Public voice of the church. As a church and as public voters, encourage legislative changes for laws that need to be put into place to protect victims and punish traffickers. There is power in numbers, especially in the eyes of politicians, so let your voice be heard. Research which laws your local and national government have in place concerning human trafficking. If you are unsure where to start, contact organizations like International Justice Mission. They have been leaders in the fight for justice through legislation advocacy. When the opportunity comes, have people sign petitions for law changes and declare your desire for justice. Even if things don't change immediately, we must persevere and keep the issue on the public agenda. One of Wilberforce's greatest traits was his persevering spirit that would not give up, even after years of defeat, which kept this issue always before the British parliament.

Create neighborhood watch programs. As an individual believer, a small group, or as a church, help bring the community together by raising awareness on this issue and creating neighborhood watch programs. Here are some signs to look for in human tracking:

- *Living and Working Conditions.* Victims of trafficking often live and work in poor conditions.

They may work long hours with little or no pay; have inadequate food, water, and shelter; and may have limited or no access to medical care. They may also live in overcrowded, unsanitary, and unsafe living conditions.

- *Lack of Control.* Trafficking victims often have little control over their lives. They may have had their documents or identification taken from them, and they may be under the control of someone else who dictates what they do, where they go, and whom they can talk to. They may also be restricted in their ability to talk to others.

- *Physical Signs.* Trafficking victims may show signs of physical abuse such as bruises, cuts, or other injuries. They may appear fearful, tired, ill, or even malnourished.

- *Fear and Isolation.* Trafficking victims may be afraid to speak out or seek help due to fear of reprisals from their trafficker or fear of law enforcement. They may also be isolated from their families and communities.

- *Inability to Leave.* Trafficking victims may be unable to leave their situation. They may be under constant surveillance, have no money or resources, or be afraid of what will happen if they try to escape.

- *Inconsistent or False Stories.* Trafficking victims may provide inconsistent or false stories about their situation, such as where they are from, where they work, or how they arrived in their current situation.

It is important to note that not all trafficking victims will show all of these signs, and some may not show any at all. It is important to grow in awareness and report your concerns if you do suspect something. Sometimes there may be something in your spirit or gut that tells you something is not right. If you do suspect something is not right, you can call the National Human Trafficking Hotline at 1-888-373-7888.

RAISING AWARENESS

BECOME AWARE
I intentionally put "raising awareness" near the end of my list of suggestions, even though for most people it would be the top item on what we need to do. While I agree that everyone needs to begin with awareness, I have seen how awareness can actually work against you if you do not have an action plan for people to be involved with right away. In short, what I have learned is that awareness without action leads to apathy.

Here are a few simple ways to raise awareness:

Social media and blogs. An easy way to help raise awareness within your own social circles is simply by blogging or posting stories on trafficking. Many friends become aware of issues and causes simply through the articles and news reports that get posted through social media.

My friend Tara Teng, who was Miss World Canada, regularly posts on her Facebook page and on Twitter about human trafficking. On one occasion, after she posted about signs to look for to see if someone is being trafficked, a viewer realized that her father was using slave labor for the family restaurant. As difficult as it was to turn her own father in to the police, this girl knew it was the right thing to do. She called the police, who came and investigated and discovered that her father was indeed guilty of labor trafficking. They planned a raid and rescued the young men and women from their imprisonment.

Simply through a post on Facebook, Tara was able to inform her friends of the horror of trafficking, and as a result, a group of people were set free from their slavery.

Campaigns. Awareness campaigns are a great way to let the community know that the body of Christ, His church, cares for people outside of its four walls. Through walkathons and/or bike-a-thons, every age group in the church can participate, bringing the church together and becoming a witness along the way. Some of these campaigns can also be used as fundraising events that will not only raise awareness but will also collect money that can be used to support anti-trafficking organizations or aftercare centers.

Screenings. Public screenings of human trafficking films provide a great way for people from the community to become aware of this issue and become familiar with your church. It would be a movie night with a purpose.

Conferences. Hosting a conference and inviting an expert in this field such as representatives from IJM, Exodus Cry, Agape International Missions, Restore Children and Family Services, or HOPE Be Restored can help educate your church and inspire your group towards action. Also, if you are unable to host your own conference, have your congregation attend national conferences that are held throughout the year.

Arts, books, and media. Hannah More was an abolitionist during the transatlantic slave trade in the nineteenth century who wrote poems against the slave trade and encouraged other women to use their skills to spread the message of what was happening to these victims. Suddenly a group of middle-class women played a key role in raising awareness during this time period. Some of them wrote plays that portrayed the realities of what was happening; others made paintings; some wrote children's books on the issue; and others wrote articles for newspapers and churches.

RESEARCH

One way to grow in personal awareness is to research and study what is happening in terms of human trafficking within your own community. Through news reports, you can keep track of convictions and arrests connected to trafficking in your area and use that to guide your prayers. Here are some ideas to grow as a researcher:

Spiritual map. The church can map out other spiritual strongholds within the community by creating a spiritual map of your neighborhoods. Print out a map of your area and highlight areas of influence (good or bad) that need to be kept in prayer. This can be a helpful aid to the prayer-walking teams that go from your church. By mapping the neighborhood, you can see how changes are happening in your community as you continue to pray.

Specialized research. We have a research team for our justice ministry that has documented trafficking cases connected to Koreans for the past several years. They categorize their findings and turn it into a brief overview paper, which has become a helpful resource for others to learn about trafficking in South Korea. As patterns and trends come up within our research, it paves the way for us to have more specialized research available as well. For example, a common theme among young girls who end up sex trafficked in South Korea is broken family backgrounds, which led many of them to run away from home. So another research project our team is working on is the connection between runaways in Korea and trafficking. This will ultimately help families, counselors, youth pastors, and others who work with children to realize the vulnerability factors for children and what to look for to help those who may end up on the streets. It will serve as an awareness tool and a preventative tool.

GIVE TIME AND RESOURCES

Volunteer. Most aftercare centers and organizations that fight human trafficking are nonprofits with limited funding and resources. Find out which groups are in your area and offer to serve in them. We have taught English to some of the staff members and survivors for one aftercare center. During Christmas, we threw a party and gave gifts, thanking the staff members for the wonderful work that they were doing. We have had others volunteer their language and translation skills to help Southeast Asian women who were trafficked into South Korea but who were in need of help with the Korean language, and filling out the legal documentation, and for applying for work permits. And for other groups, we have taught the women guitar, helped clean their offices, and sometimes just baked some cookies. These small acts of kindness and service have allowed us to build a good relationship of trust with many aftercare centers in South Korea. Please be understanding and gracious if groups do not take you up on your offer to volunteer because of the sensitivity of the work they are involved with. The protection and privacy of their victims must be guarded well. If you or your church are limited with resources, simply offer your services to support and help other groups that are already in this battle.

Give financially. Last but not least, you can always give your finances to support groups that are doing the good work of rescue, restoration, and intervention. A little money can go a long way in helping people who have lived through this nightmare of human trafficking. Ten dollars in Cambodia will allow a rescued girl to be in a shelter for over a week. A few hundred dollars can help a stateless student get a college education and a whole new world of opportunities. There are many great organizations to give to, and I've provided a list of some of them in Appendix 1 of this book. Prayerfully seek how you and your church can give generously and make a world of difference in the lives of many.

Provide vocational training. I often challenge those in our ministry who own their own businesses to provide vocational training to survivors of trafficking. I've been encouraged to see a number of them respond generously.

Here is the story of Jonathan who is a co-founder and owner of Vatos, one of the most popular Korean-Mexican fusion restaurants in Korea:

> "The most difficult step is probably converting inspiration into tangible action, because as you try to act on your newly discovered convictions, you will inevitably run into unexpected real-life problems. It was the same in our case.
>
> "As a restaurant group, we thought the most effective contribution we could make was to open up employment opportunities for the victims of trafficking. Sounds simple enough, but as our first couple of cases showed, there were underlying hurdles to overcome. Some of the victims were trafficked to Korea illegally or had visas given out for the modeling and entertainment industry. Solving the visa issue to give them legal work status was difficult. But even if they were able to clear this first obstacle, it was evident that many of them had no real training because of living on their own in Korean

society. With many having very limited Korean language skills, they had no knowledge of how to carry out basic activities of independent life, such as paying utility fees, opening bank accounts, or even signing up for a cell-phone service. They had been living in an entrapped environment, where basic freedoms and tasks that we take for granted in our everyday lives had been taken away. So when they were thrown back into real society, they were like a fish out of water. And as a company, we didn't have the resources to give them the necessary one-on-one support that they needed to acclimate to Korean society.

"There were some successful cases in the early stages though. Survivors who came from shelters and organizations that gave them exposure to work training and internships through their co-op programs thrived and had an easier time adjusting. The restaurant business has a lot of areas where you have to directly interact with people, whether it's with a fellow employee or with customers. Very early on we discovered that self-confidence was a huge factor in determining success rates, and confidence was something that many of the survivors had to build up over time.

"Another group that we see frequently at our company is women who come to Korea through arranged-marriage brokers. As we all know, the international marriage-arrangement industry is shady at best. Unfortunately, many women are arranged into abusive marriages, but they are powerless because they do not speak the language, and their husbands hold their visa status hostage. To make matters worse, these women face an inherent problem of racism in Korean society, which makes finding employment with law-abiding working hours and wages difficult. These women are typically from Southeast Asia, and there is an increasing number of international marriage brides in Korea.

"Vatos now has a growing group of Filipina employees who have used the company as a safe haven to not only collaborate but also to gather information and resources to help their fellow sisters' situations. By providing a stable working environment with a fair living wage and the opportunity for advancement, these women thrive, with many of them being our longest tenured employees and in leadership positions. One of our Filipina employees recently texted me a picture of a gray, two-story house with green picket windows. She explained that she had been saving money from her monthly salary to buy this house in the Philippines, and that is where her family is going to move to once her husband retires.

"The idea that we can pursue something greater and contribute to kingdom work even though we are just a company that sells tacos and burritos helps us stay grounded and not get caught up with the pitfalls of today's business world.

"Personally, I think the most important takeaway from Pastor Eddie and his justice ministry is how he challenged me to think differently about my role in pursuing justice. He showed me that every single one of us, no matter what field we work in, can and should be playing a role in bringing about justice. It is the role of a Christian to want justice for our fellow man, and we shouldn't be afraid of being uncomfortable as a church to pursue issues that others feel uneasy with, because it's about showing others what Christ looks like as we love and serve them."

This is by no means an exhaustive list of what churches can do in the fight against human trafficking, but it is a start. I hope you can use this list as a catalyst for action to get people involved. I also hope this can inspire more ideas to come out of the local church, so the universal church – the body of Christ – will one day take its rightful place on the frontlines in the fight for freedom and justice.

GROUP DISCUSSION QUESTIONS:

- Which two or three ideas from this list do you feel you could begin doing right away?

- Which two or three ideas do you think your church can be involved with?

- What will you do now to make these ideas a reality within your life and ministry?

PRAYER GUIDE:

- Ask God for wisdom, humility, and courage to take the next steps of action.

- This is spiritual warfare, so take some time to pray for protection over you, your church, and your pastor as you move into this area of justice.

- Pray for your church to be used by God to bring freedom and hope to your community.

CONCLUSION: THE TIME IS NOW

*Righteousness and justice are the foundation of
your throne; steadfast love and faithfulness go
before you.* (Psalm 89:14)

Human trafficking is now considered the sec-
ond-largest and fastest-growing illegal trafficking activity in the world.[58]

There are times to read history, and there are
times to make history.[59]

We often think that slavery is a thing of the past. Four
centuries of the transatlantic slave trade strikes us as an
unconscionable evil. But according to the President's Advisory
Council on Faith-Based and Neighborhood Partnerships, there
are more slaves today than at any other point in human history!
Let that sink in. There are actually more slaves today than
all the slaves brutally and cruelly transported from Africa for
more than four centuries!

---

58   "What is Human Trafficking?" *Human Rights Commission: https://tinyurl.com/
       bdcdaftk* (March 14, 2023).
59   Batstone, *Not for Sale,* 18.

Horrifically, a slave today is cheaper in today's dollars than slaves of the past. Whereas it once cost the equivalent of $40,000 to enslave a human being, today it's a mere $90. According to one study, a single prostitute can earn her pimp up to $250,000 a year minimum. Such lucrative numbers are more profitable than the sale of drugs or guns. It makes trafficking humans one of the highest-grossing industries in the world.

According to the Gospel Coalition, almost 40 percent of all incidents investigated by U.S. law enforcement agencies between 2008 and 2010 "involved prostitution of a child or child sexual exploitation."[60] And a disproportionate amount of child trafficking takes place in Asia where sex tourists – including those from wealthier Asian nations like Japan and South Korea – visit poorer countries where children are captured, sold, and exploited for profit.

Edmund Burke has been credited with saying, "All that is necessary for the triumph of evil is for good men to do nothing." After seeing the magnitude and scope of the evil of human trafficking, we can easily become discouraged to the point of feeling utterly helpless to do anything when we see how big and dark the situation is in our world today. But there is hope, because light is always greater than darkness. A law of nature in the physical world points us to the greater reality in the spiritual realm. As light is always greater than darkness, love is stronger than hatred. In the end, God will right all wrongs.

Thus, on the flip side of that, we can say, "All that is necessary for good to triumph is for good men to do something." That "something" is what this book is about – doing the good works of Jesus so His kingdom can expand and His throne be established in every nation of this earth.

---

60   Joe Carter, "Where Sex Trafficking Occurs in America," *TGC: U.S. Edition: https://tinyurl.com/yc4n8kd8* (March 14, 2023).

WHO WILL LEAD?

In his first policy address as attorney general, Alberto Gonzales called trafficking one of the most pernicious moral evils in the world today. As Attorney General Gonzales stated, "This abomination does not exist only in other lands; it exists right here on our shores. Today its victims are usually aliens, many of them women and children, smuggled into our country and held in bondage, treated as commodities, stripped of their humanity."[61]

In 2011, CNN launched their Freedom Project, which is their coverage on human trafficking around the world. This was unusual for them because they are normally just a breaking-news network, but they decided to utilize their global resources and influence to expose this evil and influence change. Here is the message from one of their first promotional clips explaining why they started The Freedom Project:

Around the world, millions of men, women, and children are being bought and sold. Enough is enough. It's time to put an end to modern-day slavery. Today we launch The CNN Freedom Project. All year with CNN's unmatched resources, we go beyond the borders to tackle slavery head-on, to untangle the criminal web that trades in human life, to give victims a voice, to bring captors to justice and keep government officials to their word. The victims can't walk away and neither will we. It's time to put modern-day slavery out of business, and CNN has joined the fight to bring hope and freedom with The CNN Freedom Project.[62]

That is wonderful, isn't it? It was so inspiring. Yet, it also left me feeling a bit awkward when I first watched this. Later, I realized why I felt this way. It's because this should have been the

---

61   The U.S. Attorney General Report 2006, *"Prepared Remarks of Attorney General Alberto Gonzales, Hoover Institution Board of Overseers Conference,"* *The United States Department of Justice – Archives: https://tinyurl.com/y2uxd4kt* (February 28, 2005).

62   The first commercial advertising CNN's Freedom Project.

declaration from the church! That should be our message to the world, but we have allowed everyone else to take the lead in this fight for justice, freedom, and righteousness. It was then that I gained a stronger conviction of the church's role in this movement.

If we, the church, are not the preeminent leaders in this fight for justice and in the demonstrations of mercy to the oppressed, then we are allowing the world to look more like Jesus than we do.

It is a picture of Jesus when we care for the weak, the oppressed, the outcast, and the vulnerable. It is time for the church to rise up out of its apathy and slumber and be the leaders and the hands and feet of Christ that we were created to be. We are the light of the world, and where there is light, darkness will flee, for light is always greater than darkness. It is our call to love the oppressed and the outcast, for these are the ones that Jesus loves so deeply.

WHAT WILL WE LEAVE BEHIND?

I do not want to leave this great evil as an inheritance to my children's generation. We must rise up to end this injustice, and it must begin today. History will remember and honor those who fought for justice. History has honored the men and women who have risen to the challenges of their generation. We honor Harriet Tubman for freeing thousands of slaves through the underground railroad. History honors William Wilberforce, the abolitionist who brought an end to the slave trade after forty-six years of fighting. We honor them because they fought for freedom. But what if it were happening today? What if you lived in their time period? What would you do? Stand by and do nothing or join them in their fight? History records and remembers those who fought for justice.

Something David Batstone wrote woke me up to this situation like nothing else I've read. These were the words that awakened this sleeping soldier:

"There are times to read history, and there are times to make history. We live right now at one of those epic moments in the fight for human freedom. We no longer have to wonder how we might respond to our moment of truth. We are on the stage, and we can change the winds of history with our actions. Future generations will look back to judge our choices and be inspired or disappointed."[63]

You have been given liberty, knowledge, wealth, influence, position, and power for such a time as this. There is a time to read history, and there's a time to make history. Now is the time to make history and set the captives free. There is a time and a season for everything, and the time for justice is now.

GROUP DISCUSSION QUESTIONS:

- What are some new things you learned through this book study?

- What convicted you the most?

- How will your life be different now?

PRAYER GUIDE:

- Pray for a global awakening to happen in the church and for the church to lead the way in our pursuit of justice for the oppressed.

- Pray for your church to be a change agent in your community – shining light, being salt, giving love.

- Pray for the injustice of human trafficking to come to an end in our lifetime.

---

63   Batstone, *Not for Sale,* 18.

APPENDIX 1

RESOURCES FOR FREEDOM AND JUSTICE

SERMONS

- Visit my website for sermons on human trafficking and justice: www.eddiebyun.com

ORGANIZATIONS

- Some great organizations are worthy of your prayers and support:
- Restore Children and Family Services https://restorechildren.org/
- Agape International Missions http://agapewebsite.org/
- HOPE Be Restored http://www.hopeberestored.org/
- International Justice Mission http://ijm.org/
- NightLight International http://www.nightlight-international.com/
- Ratanak International www.ratanak.org
- ZOE International http://zoechildren.org/

BOOKS

- *Amazing Grace in the Life of William Wilberforce* by John Piper

- *Deepening the Soul for Justice* by Bethany H. Hoang

- *Ending Human Trafficking* by Shayne Moore, Sandra Morgan, and Kimberly McOwen Yim

- *False Justice: Unveiling the Truth About Social Justice* by Stuart Greaves

- *Generous Justice: How God's Grace Makes Us Just* by Timothy Keller

- *God in a Brothel* by Daniel Walker

- *God, Justice, and Society* by Jonathan Burnside

- *God of Justice* by Abraham George and Nikki A. Toyama-Szeto

- *Good News About Injustice* by Gary Haugen

- *The Hole in Our Gospel* by Richard Stearns

- *Human Trafficking: A Global Perspective* by Louise Shelley

- *The Just Church* by Jim Martin

- *Just Courage* by Gary Haugen

- *Justice in Love* by Nicholas Wolterstorff

- *Justice: Rights and Wrongs* by Nicholas Wolterstorff

- *The Natashas* by Victor Malarek

- *Not for Sale* by David Batstone

- *Sex Trafficking: Inside the Business of Modern Slavery* by Siddharth Kara

- *Vulnerable: Rethinking Human Trafficking* by Raleigh Sadler

FILMS

- *Save My Seoul*
- *At the End of Slavery: The Battle for Justice in Our Time* (IJM)
- *Nefarious: Merchant of Souls* (Exodus Cry)
- *Raised on Porn: The New Sex Ed* (Exodus Cry)
- *Beyond Fantasy* (Exodus Cry)

APPENDIX 2

CASE STUDY ON KOREA

**A Glimpse into South Korea's Domestic and
International Human-Trafficking Issues
(HOPE Be Restored Research Team)[64]**

INTRODUCTION

Human trafficking is a form of modern-day slavery. Current estimates have more than fifty million victims of human trafficking today.[65] There are 166 countries reportedly affected by human trafficking either by being a source, a transit, or a destination country.[66] Additionally, the International Labour Organization (ILO) reports that 4.5 million people are trafficked with the intent of being used for sexual exploitation. An overwhelming majority of these victims end up in the sex industry in the Pacific and Asia.[67] These statistics have caused HOPE Be Restored, a Seoul-based organization, to take a stand against this injustice and pursue the abolishment of human trafficking both in and out of South Korea.

---

64 Contributors: Genevieve Pierce, Cynthia Goss, Richard Biggs, Ben Spink, Michelle Constantine, and Rebekah McNay. Editing/Formatting: Genevieve Pierce and Cynthia Goss.

65 Fitzgerald, "How Modern Slavery Survives Across the World," (March 21, 2023).

66 "Child Trafficking by Country 2023," *World Population Review: https://world-populationreview.com/* (March 15, 2023).

67 "21 million people are now victims of forced labour, ILO says," *International Labour Organization* (June 1, 2012): *https://tinyurl.com/3krxsavj* (March 15, 2023).

As defined by the United Nations (UN), human trafficking involves any act of recruiting, transporting, transferring, harboring, or receiving a person through a use of force, coercion, or other means for the purpose of exploiting them.[68] HOPE Be Restored is working under this definition of human trafficking and, for the purpose of clarification, for incorporating prostitution – whether voluntary or forced – into our data. Though slightly controversial, the admittance of prostitution is crucial because those who are trafficked in and out of South Korea are primarily involved in the sex industry. Differentiating between voluntary and forced prostitution is nearly impossible due to the nature of the industry. Therefore, since prostitution is illegal in South Korea, HOPE Be Restored has chosen to include all data associated with prostitution.

This report will primarily focus on three major aspects of South Korea's human-trafficking network and its sex industry. These focuses are:

- Koreans trafficked out of South Korea.

- Foreigners trafficked into South Korea.

- Koreans trafficked within South Korea.

A BRIEF HISTORY OF HUMAN TRAFFICKING IN AND OUT OF SOUTH KOREA

In the twentieth century, Korea was the country of origin for many migrant workers around the world. Koreans sought migrant work in pursuit of opportunity and highly valued foreign currency. The sex industry was one of its exports, sending women to conflict zones so they could offer their services to military personnel, largely servicing U.S. soldiers fighting in the Vietnam War.[69]

---

68   "Toolkit to Combat Trafficking in Persons": *https://tinyurl.com/mpbpnp3h* (March 15, 2023).

69   Dong-Hoon Seol, "International Sex Trafficking in Women in Korea: Its Causes, Consequences and Countermeasures," *Asian Center for Women's Studies,* Vol. 10, No. 2 (2004): 8.

In the 1990s, due to the boom in the Korean economy, more money than ever began to flow through the country. This increase in capital brought a higher standard of living and an increase in expendable income, an unimaginable luxury of ages past. With this economic boost, the roles of migrant workers reversed. Instead of flowing out of the country, they began to flow in. As of 1996, Korea has "changed from a country of origin for international sex trafficking in women to become a host country."[70] The increase in demand generated a steady supply and vice versa, confirming that the Korean sex industry is a market-based economy that exists on the principle of supply and demand with high profits and little risk. Thus, the sex industry in South Korea is a highly profitable and strong harvesting ground for imported and exported sex workers.

KOREANS TRAFFICKED OUT OF SOUTH KOREA

South Korean women are reported to be the most trafficked nationals into the United States, Japan, and Australia. The countries are rated on a four-tier scale – Tier 1 being the highest – according to how they comply with The Victims of Trafficking and Violence Protection Act of 2000 passed by the U.S. Department of State.

UNITED STATES

The United States is ranked as a Tier 1 country in the U.S. Department of State's TIP 2012 Report. "A Tier 1 ranking indicates that a government has acknowledged the existence of human trafficking, has made efforts to address the problem, and meets the TVPA's (Trafficking Victims Protection Act of 2000) minimum standards. . . . Tier 1 represents a responsibility rather than a reprieve."[71] The U.S. Attorney General's report for Fiscal

---

70 Dong-Hoon Seol, "International Sex Trafficking in Women in Korea," 8.

71 "Trafficking in Persons Report – 2012," *U.S. Department of State, 2012: http:// www.state.gov/j/tip/rls/tiprpt/2012/* (March 16, 2023).

Year 2005 says, "The highest populations of victims originated in Korea (23.5%), Thailand (11.7%), Peru (10.0%), and Mexico (9.6%)," but this is within the context of certification of victims under the TVPA.[72] Korea had the biggest population of those victims who were reported and then subsequently certified. It cannot be determined how good this measure is as an indication of the overall situation. Furthermore, the same report for 2010 showed that Korea had dropped to fourth place.

The United States views prostitution as illegal and takes legal action to eradicate the sex industry, yet it is one of the largest destinations for Korean trafficking. As of 2007, there were approximately three hundred thousand Koreans illegally in the United States according to the U.S. Office of Immigration Statistics. The areas that have the largest number of Korean-operated sex establishments are the northeastern United States, Dallas, San Francisco, and Los Angeles.[73] These areas are densely populated with illegal Koreans and have been the focus of many FBI investigations regarding the sex industry. In Los Angeles alone there is an estimated total of ten thousand Korean women working in the sex industry.

The U.S. law enforcement reported that in the major areas, such as Los Angeles and San Francisco, there was an estimate of 345 venues owned by Koreans that offered sexual services. According to Barry Tang, who is part of the Immigration and Customs Enforcement (ICE) attached to the U.S. Department of Homeland Security in South Korea, said, "There's a highly organized logical network between Korea and the United States with recruiters, brokers, intermediaries, taxi drivers,

---

72   "Attorney General's Annual Report to Congress on U.S. Government Activities to Combat Trafficking in Persons Fiscal Year 2005," *U.S. Department of Justice; 2006: https://tinyurl.com/4bfdcdaf* (March 17, 2023), 6.

73   Timothy C. Lim, "Migrant Korean women in the U.S. commercial sex industry: an examination of the causes and dynamics of cross-border sexual exploitation," *Journal of Research in Gender Studies,* Vol. 4, Issue 1, *Gale Academic Onefile: https://tinyurl.com/3ye34dbv* (March 17, 2023).

and madams."[74] Though it is extremely difficult to have a firm number on how many Koreans are actually trafficked into the United States for the purpose of sexual exploitation, it is safe to assume that no matter the exact number, thousands of Koreans are being sexually exploited in the United States annually.

CASE STUDY

Sex trafficking victims rarely receive the opportunity to tell their story. Therefore, when the *San Francisco Gate* did a three-part series on a Korean college student, You Mi Kim, who revealed she had been smuggled into California by sex traffickers, people began to listen.[75]

Kim came from a poor family, but when she went to college and was offered a credit card, she saw the opportunity to impress her friends. She spent lavishly on clothes, cosmetics, and entertaining her newfound friends, but was $10,000 in debt after a year. The credit card company cut off her credit, and she was obliged to take out loans from loan sharks at 25 percent interest to repay the debt. She dropped out of college and found work, but even with that, her spending behavior did not change. She acquired another credit card to pay back the debt and continued to go to the loan sharks. A year later, she was $40,000 in debt.

She considered prostituting herself in bars to repay the mounting debt, but she could not stomach it, and she thought her prayers had been answered when she saw an internet ad promising, "Work in an American room salon. Make $10,000 a month. Very gentle. No touching. No second round."[76] She figured she could work for six months and come back to re-enroll in college. Because she didn't

74 Meredith May, "SEX TRAFFICKING: San Francisco Is a Major Center for International Crime Networks That Smuggle and Enslave: Part 1," *San Francisco Gate* (October 6, 2006): *https://tinyurl.com/3hv238ss* (March 18, 2023).

75 Meredith May, "Diary of a Sex Slave / The Story," *San Francisco Gate* (October 9, 2006): *https://tinyurl.com/s4psa4zr* (March 18, 2023).

76 Meredith May, "A Youthful Mistake, Part 2," *San Francisco Gate* (October 8, 2006): *https://tinyurl.com/yhmjszpz* (March 18, 2023).

have a passport or a visa, the agent said she would have to pay $7,000 in travel expenses, which she could repay with her earnings. She was unsure but desperate to be freed of her debt, so she agreed.

Unexpectedly, her flight was bound for Mexico. Her handlers explained that it was because she didn't have a visa, and it was easier to get into the United States this way. She transferred to Tijuana and was driven across the border, eventually arriving in Los Angeles. Her new boss there informed her that her travel expenses had come to $11,000. Exhausted from a week of nerve-wracking travel, she agreed.

Her boss drove her to several room salons for job interviews, but she was turned down at all of them. In the end, he offered her an ultimatum: pay back the money she owed for her travel and accommodation expenses or work for his wife's outcall service – as a prostitute. With her $40,000 debt waiting for her at home, she had no choice but to accept. On her first day she was called out three times, but she did not keep any of the money – half went to paying her debt, and the other half went to the outcall service.

She was awkward and inexperienced, so she couldn't keep her customers, and after two months, she still owed $6,000 to her traffickers. They got impatient and sold her for $7,200. Kim ended up in a brothel in a residential neighborhood. At the end of her twelve-hour shift on her first day there, she had had sex with fourteen men. After three months of being bounced around from one establishment to another in Los Angeles, she was free of her debt to the traffickers, but she still had the debt in Korea, and she had incurred $10,000 in legal fees when she was arrested for prostitution. She was free, but she could not leave. She had no choice but to carry on, and she moved to San Francisco where the pay was better.

For the next four months, Kim would service more than twelve men a day, six days a week, in San Francisco's notorious Tenderloin district. She became unrecognizable as a person – from being shy and nervous, she was now bouncy and playful with her customers.

She hoped to get repeat customers who believed she enjoyed spending time with them, which would make it faster to get herself out of the hole. And it worked. After four months, she had paid off all her debts in the United States and Korea. It was over.

But she couldn't go home. The shame of what she had done and the trouble she had caused her family prevented her from returning to Korea. She received a T-1 visa, and she currently resides in San Francisco, working as a waitress. She finds it difficult to make friends, and she keeps her face down in public in case one of her clients recognizes her. She has lingering health problems, and the gynecologist has told her that she has a high chance of contracting cervical cancer. She is twenty-three years old.

JAPAN

Prostitution is illegal in Japan, but it is still tolerated. Japan was ranked as a Tier-2 country in the U.S. Department of State's TIP 2022 Report.[77] There are from 130,000 to 150,000 foreign women in Japan's $83 billion sex industry.[78] According to the Japanese Ministry of Justice, there are estimated to be 6,000 to 7,000 Koreans documented to be working in the sex industry under the entertainment visa.[79] Entertainment visas are the primary way in which foreign women are brought into countries in order to cover up the sex industry. According to Polaris Project Japan's Hotline, "About 30% of S.O.S calls made to the hotline since 2005 were by Koreans, making them the most targeted foreign victims."[80]

AUSTRALIA

Australia was ranked as a Tier-1 country in the U.S. Department

---

77   "2022 Trafficking in Persons Report: Japan," *U.S. Department of State: https://www.state.gov/reports/2022-trafficking-in-persons-report/japan/* (March 18, 2023).

78   Donna M. Hughes, "The Demand for Victims of Sex Trafficking," *Women's Studies, University of Rhode Island 2005: https://tinyurl.com/268ycbv3* (March 18, 2023), 50.

79   Ibid.

80   Sim Guk-by, "Korean victims of sex trafficking in Japan receive renewed attention," *Korea Herald* (updated June 29, 2012): *https://tinyurl.com/yszrkrxb* (March 18, 2023).

of State's TIP 2022 Report.[81] In Australia, figures and studies show that the majority of trafficked people are being brought in from Asian countries and a large number of them from South Korea specifically. According to one study, "between the 2003-04 and 2009-10 financial years . . . 26% [of trafficking in persons, investigations, and assessments] involved South Korean nationals."[82] The Australian Federal Police clearly acknowledge that "Australia is primarily a destination country for people trafficked from Asia, particularly Thailand, Korea, the Philippines and Malaysia."[83] Unfortunately, there is not much solid research on specific numbers of cases of human trafficking in Australia, but most sources claim a relatively low number. This is largely due to the fact that in Australia, according to the Prostitution Act of 1992, prostitution is considered legal and does not fall under what they consider to be human trafficking.[84] Under the same act, it is also stated that all brothels and the people involved must be registered with the government.

However, if the woman does identify herself as being a victim of human trafficking specifically, the Australian government provides many options in the form of aid and protection. For example, as of July 2009, victims are offered an opportunity to acquire a Witness Protection visa (which is permanent and includes their family) if they help in the prosecution of criminals within the industry.[85]

---

81   "2022 Trafficking in Persons Report: Australia," *U.S. Department of State:* *https://tinyurl.com/ycksy67b* (March 18, 2023).

82   "Human Trafficking Working Group – Statistics and Other Data," *The University of Queensland* (2011): *http://www.law.uq.edu.au/human-trafficking-statistics* (September 12, 2011).

83   *https://www.afp.gov.au/what-we-do/crime-types/human-trafficking.*

84   "Republication of the Prostitution Act of 1992," *ACT Parliamentary Counsel; Australian Government* (December 12, 2011): *http://www.legislation.act.gov.au/a/1992-64/current/pdf/1992-64.pdf* (March 18, 2023).

85   Lisa Mary Connell, "Human Trafficking for Sexual Exploitation in Australia: The Deafening Silence on Demand," *Centre for Strategic Economic Studies* (Melbourne: Victoria University, April 2012): *https://vuir.vu.edu.au/21449/1/Lisa_Mary_Connell.pdf* (March 18, 2023).

FOREIGNERS TRAFFICKED INTO SOUTH KOREA
It is possible that the apex of the issue of Koreans trafficking foreigners into Korea lies in the discrepancies of the issuance and application of the E-6 visa. This specific visa issued to foreigners is labeled the Arts/Entertainment visa. This is issued with the understanding that recipients are in Korea to pursue careers within that realm. However, often the traffickers have sought and received this visa for individuals whom they promised entertainment careers (sometimes in the K-pop industry), and upon arrival, said individuals were forced into sexual servitude and coerced by their visa situation, which requires participation in the arts as the only means of making money while in the country.

This first became an issue with the importation of Russian women, mostly to camp towns outside U.S. Army bases. However, in 2003 the South Korean government stopped issuing the E-6 visa to the Russian women. Recently, there has been a noticeable increase in the issuance of the E-6 visa, only this time to Filipino women. The book *Exposing the Price Tag* remarks, "Since [2003], a growing number of Filipino women have been issued the same E-6 visa to gain entry to Korea, replacing Russian dancers."[86] Furthermore, a recent article in the *Korea Times* states that while there has been a pleasant restriction to the E-6 visa since the time it was being used to bring Russian women over to Korea, it is now being used to authorize Filipino women to work the "juicy bars" near these army bases. These are run on the pretense that soldiers buy glasses of juice in order to spend time with, flirt, and dance with the women. "Those women who fail to meet a quota for juice sales are often subject to 'bar fines,' meaning they are told to sell their body to account for the shortfall."[87] This highlights the crux of the

---

86   *Exposing the Price Tag* (Dassi Hamkke Center, Seoul, South Korea, 2012), 125.
87   Kim Young-jin, "Outside U.S. bases, former bar workers fight sex trafficking," *National, The Korea Times* (updated February 27, 2012): *https://www.koreatimes. co.kr/www/news/nation/2012/02/116_105839.html* (March 20, 2023).

issue with the E-6 visa. With the requisite to obtain the visa being "for those seeking to make profit with performance," the definition of what "performance" entails is unnecessarily ambiguous. It is clear that until the definition is clarified as to what qualifies as appropriate "performance," this incongruity will enable the genre of exploitation.

There were 4,970 E-6 visa holders in Korea in 2009 – 77 percent of them were women.[88] The Korean Ministry of Culture, Sports, and Tourism (MCST), the government ministry that oversees the E-6 visa, has been "criticized for automatically approving visa applicants through local entertainment companies. For example, it does not monitor workplaces employing E-6 workers."[89] This is not a new situation. Five years earlier, in the ILO's 2004 report on "Human Trafficking for Sexual Exploitation in Japan," it said that the Japanese Immigration Bureau "plans to review the requirements for the Entertainment Visa and/or examine more closely the qualifications of applicants as entertainers."[90] While it cannot be said that the Korean government has abetted the trafficking of entertainers, certainly its negligence in screening the applicants for E-6 visas, as it would do stringently for any other visa application, is noteworthy.

KOREANS TRAFFICKED WITHIN SOUTH KOREA

Though many hail from other nations, a large part of the 270,000 prostitutes in Korea are Korean.[91] While the reasons for their entry into the industry may vary, most are deceived by friends or pimps, and others are "sold" because of debt.[92]

88   "South Korea: Disposable Labour: Rights of Migrant Workers in South Korea," *Amnesty International* (October 21, 2009): *https://www.amnesty.org/en/documents/asa25/001/2009/en/* (March 20, 2023), 80.

89   Ibid.

90   "Human Trafficking for Sexual Exploitation in Japan," *International Labour Office* (2004): *https://tinyurl.com/bdcyk7yn* (March 20, 2023), 44.

91   "Survey of the National Status of Sex Trafficking," *Ministry of Gender Equality and Family (MOGEF)* (2007), xvii.

92   "Survey of the National Status of Sex Trafficking" (*MOGEF*) (2010), 8.

Of these women, 80 percent are victims of physical violence – seven out of ten having attempted suicide.[93] With ninety-four million cases of prostitution occurring every year, prostitution is a 14-trillion-won (Korean currency; 10.8 million U.S. dollars) industry in Korea alone.[94]

The 2004 Act on the Prevention of Sexual Traffic and Protection of Victims changed the face of the prostitution industry in Korea. The number of prostituted women fell from 330,000 in 2002 to 270,000 by 2007, and the value of the industry plunged from over 24 trillion won (approximately 18 billion U.S. dollars) in 2002 to 14 trillion won (approximately 10.7 billion U.S. dollars) in 2007.[95] It is surmised, however, that the 2004 Act served to drive prostitution further underground, with Internet prostitution seeing a 50-percent increase over the same period. Reinvented brothels, that are run out of offices and residential locations, are said to have seen a meteoric rise but are virtually untraceable.

At the ground level, enforcement of the act is key. The Lee Myung-bak administration, which took office in 2009, has shown a hawkish attitude toward prostitution by cutting funds for shelters for prostituted women and relaxing police enforcement. A prostituted woman working in a red-light district says, "I know the law has changed, but it doesn't have any real meaning."[96] A support center for prostituted women stated that "there were about 80 establishments here before 2004 Act, . . . and when the police started enforcing the law, the number dropped to about 50. Now it's back up to 60 or 70."[97]

---

93 "Their Choice," Promotional video for prostitution prevention campaign (*MOGEF*) (2012).

94 "Survey of the National Status of Sex Trafficking" (*MOGEF*) (2007), xix.

95 Ibid., xxii.

96 Kim Ki-tae, "14 years in hell," *No. South Korea Prostitution Report 889, Hani Online (Korea)* (December 12, 2011): *http://h21.hani.co.kr/arti/society/society_general/30944.html* (March 20, 2023).

97 Ibid.

The workers in Korean RLDs are primarily teenage runaways. Runaways often become targets for prostitution. Statistics state,[98]

- There are an estimated two hundred thousand runaways in Korea.

- A quarter of all runaway girls admit to having given sexual favors for money.

- The average age of running away from home for the first time is thirteen.

- Runaways are getting younger: between 2010 and 2011, the total number of reported runaways increased by 44 percent, but the number of runaways under thirteen increased by 148 percent.

CASE STUDY

The story below is an actual account taken from the book *Exposing the Price Tag*. Yujin Lee was lured into the trafficking industry when her father's health took a turn for the worse, and she felt obligated to help support her family. She went to a fortune teller and learned that she could make good money at a dabang,[99] and that she would even gain a two-million-won (one month's salary) advance payment. She learned after starting that the job required sexual intercourse; she complied because she needed the money desperately. She says,

> "I could not bear it, so when the first month was over, I ran away. The owner of Byul Dabang called me saying, 'How could you leave without telling

---

98 "Runaway families – Dangerous Cohabitation," *Chu Cheog 60bun* (추적60분 – *60 Minute Investigation), KBS* (aired July 11, 2012): *https://tinyurl.com/334ydemb* (September 3, 2012).

99 Dabangs are teahouses specializing in home delivery that are notorious for providing sexual service. Since they are officially categorized as a restaurant or entertainment business and can legally hire teenagers, dabangs are a common entry point into the sex trade for underage girls (*Exposing the Price Tag*, 145).

me? It has been fifteen days since you left, so you owe me damages of 2,300,000 won. Combined with your other debts, the total you now owe me is 5,600,000 won. If you want to quit, you'd better pay me 5,600,000 won.'

"I said, 'I'm sorry for leaving without saying anything, but I received one month's payment of 2,000,000 won as an advance payment, and I worked for a month. How could I owe you 5,600,000 won?'

"The owner threatened me. 'If you don't bring the money, I will sue you for fraud and tell your parents.' I knew this was unfair, but I was so afraid that my parents would find out."[100]

Lee's story goes on to detail her movement from dabang to dabang, the abusive treatment she received from owners and customers alike, her virtual imprisonment in the industry, and her ever-increasing debt, which eventually amounted to an astounding sixteen million won. Unfortunately, Lee's story is not unique; like Kim in San Francisco, this method of debt incursion is a very common form of manipulation to keep young Korean women hostage in the sex trade.

CONCLUSION

Nestled nicely between Southeast Asia and North America, South Korea is an ideal hub across one of the world's largest human-trafficking routes. Whether as traffickers, pimps, or victims, Koreans are certainly playing an active role in human

---

100 *Exposing the Price Tag,* 49-50.

trafficking internationally and domestically. Many Korean women, such as Kim and Lee, have found themselves in financial trouble and lured into prostitution under false pretenses while others have turned to it in desperation. Through generous distribution and trouble-free access to E-6 visas, foreigners are easily brought into Korea and lost within a convoluted and constantly changing system.

Korea was recently downgraded to a Tier-2 country on the U.S. Department of State's TIP Report.[101] The general rates of prostitution have been reportedly lower over the last few years in South Korea; however, these positive claims are not particularly evident on the streets. This leaves observers with the impression that the Korean government is simply complying to international standards without actually enforcing any tangible reforms to eradicate and prevent human trafficking and prostitution within its borders. An example of this situation can be seen in Korea's efforts against prostitution. Though prostitution is considered illegal, and there are penalties for violators, there are few firm attempts of enforcement. This lack of enforcement has allowed the industry to thrive within and out of Korea.

The global sex industry and human trafficking go hand in hand; without one, the other cannot live, and vice versa. This is the same for the supply and demand. In order to combat this difficult issue, there needs to be a lower demand and a cut in supply. Therefore, international awareness and government assertiveness are key to this issue and the only true hope for abolishment. This report simply begins to breach this topic. HOPE Be Restored seeks to open the dialogue and continually pursue the eradication of human trafficking.

For more information regarding HOPE Be Restored, please visit www.hopeberestored.org.

---

101 "2022 Trafficking in Persons Report: South Korea," *U.S. Department of State: https://www.state.gov/reports/2022-trafficking-in-persons-report/south-korea/.*

ABOUT THE AUTHOR

Eddie Byun has spent twenty-five years pastoring and teaching in the United States, Canada, Australia, and South Korea. He is the author of the award-winning book *Justice Awakening (A Light in Darkness)*, and also *Praying for Your Pastor*, and *Praying for Your Missionary*. He is also the executive producer of *Save My Seoul*, an award-winning documentary on trafficking in South Korea. Currently, he is director of the Doctor of Ministry Program and associate professor of Christian Ministry at Talbot School of Theology and Biola University.

Connect with Eddie Byun

www.eddiebyun.com

Facebook.com/eddiebyun

Twitter: @eddiebyun

Made in the USA
Monee, IL
21 June 2024

60287937R00105